NINJA DATING SKILLS:

What You Wish You Would Have Learned in High Scho0l

NINJA DATING SKILLS:

WHAT YOU WISH YOU WOULD HAVE LEARNED IN HIGH SCHOOL

MATTHEW COOPER

Ninja Skills Publishing

2014

Ninja Skills Books

The information in this book has been carefully researched, and all efforts have been made to ensure accuracy. The author and publisher assume no responsibility for any injuries suffered or damages or losses incurred during or as a result of following this information. All information should be carefully studied and clearly understood before taking any action based on the information or advice in this book. You assume full responsibility for the consequences of your own actions. If you can't agree to these terms, do not turn the page.

First Printing: 2014
ISBN:0615951287
ISBN-13:978-0615951287
Ninja Skills Publishing
203 E. Jordan Ridge Blvd.
Saratoga Springs, Utah 84045
www.ninjadatingskills.com
Ordering Information:
Special discounts are available on quantity purchases by corporations, associations, educators, and others. For details, contact the publisher at the above listed address.
U.S. trade bookstores and wholesalers: Please contact:
Ninja Skills Publishing
Phone: (435) 572-0852 or email: info@ninjadatingskills.com

DEDICATION

This book is dedicated to my children. I have worked to *"Become the change you wish to see in the world."* I believe that I have become the dad that I always wanted to be. This is also dedicated to all of my friends and family that supported me in this endeavor. See. I told you I could do it!

CONTENTS

INTRODUCTION

Everyone has a dream, even if that dream is to have a full belly and a safe place to sleep at night.

Dreaming for me is a part of daily life. My belly is full regularly and I sleep well and more safely than some. However, life is so much more than these basics. Life to me is about fulfillment. Fulfillment, to me, is to constantly grow and improve myself.

Everyone has had a rough life. Some people's idea of a rough life is different than others. I know my life is nowhere near as difficult as, say one of the wounded warriors from our Nation's military, or someone who has become a quadriplegic after living part of their life healthy.

However, I have had some rough experiences in my life. I recognize that we all have had our tough experiences and life lessons that have made us into the people we are today.

This book: *Ninja Dating Skills*, and the material that is covered in these pages, represents some of the hard learned life lessons that no one ever taught me when I was growing up.

Everyone would like to have a manual on what to do to have more success in life. The *Self-Help* section of your local bookstore is full of books that exist to help people to have more success in life.

The main area that I wanted to have more success in, for many years, was being able to connect with and have deep and fulfilling relationships with beautiful women.

In the early years when I had this desire, *more of a drive really*, I had very little success with meeting and even less success dating women. I didn't know what to do, who to talk to, what to say or even how to say it. It was horrible.

This confusion came to me as I was thrown back into the *"Dating Game"* after my wife, of 15 years, left me for her own reasons and we got divorced. I had all of my kids living with me. I had no social life.

I had been married for 15 years and was clueless about how to date (how I got married in the first place is a mystery to me). My hopes and dreams for the future were shattered and I had no idea what the future held for me. I didn't know what to do.

After floundering and flailing around in that dark place of depression and misery for too long, I began to feel like I could handle a relationship again.

I attempted to use the same skills, after brushing off the accumulated dust of nearly two decades, which I had used in high school, and to get out in public and meet women. Wow. I discovered the world had changed while I had been married and raising kids.

The stuff I had used in high school was crap. I don't know how I ever got married with the pitiful skills I was using to attract and interact with women. I was lost and had no idea of where to even begin to figure out this *dating* thing.

I had been reading and studying about relationships and the psychology of women since the *divorce*, the emotional aspects of relationships and what had gone wrong in my marriage. I started to see some patterns.

I began to realize that the divorce wasn't done to me; it was done for herself, to save herself. I realized that it wasn't personal. It was survival.

I knew that I had my own issues and that I had added to the problems that lead to the divorce, and yet she made the choice. It took me years to accept her choice to get divorced and to eventually, genuinely, thank her for making it.

This lesson changed the entire way that I looked at relationships. I spent thousands of dollars on relationship programs, workshops, lectures, books and audio books, each one having a piece of the puzzle and none of them having everything that I needed.

I still don't have all of the answers. What I do have are the skills that have worked for me.

This book is the distillation of some of the principles of dating communication that have worked for me as I have learned the hard lessons of dating, from a man's perspective.

I don't claim that this will be accurate or correct from a woman's perspective.

What I have found is that men think differently than women, and most books aren't written <u>for</u> men, <u>by</u> men, from their perspective.

This isn't a book about picking up women. This is a book about the communication and the messages that you are sending out and that you are receiving constantly.

Most men are very rational and logical, especially when it comes to dating and relationships. When I was learning these things, I wish I had a handbook that would give me some ideas; some practical hints that I could use that would make it easier for me to get started back into the dating world.

I decided to take what I had learned from the dating trainings, programs and books and life experiences and distill it down into a small handbook that had enough tips and information that anyone could use to get started on understanding the dating process, and point you in the right direction when you are ready to learn more on your own.

Enjoy the journey. It **IS** worth it.

P.S. If you are looking for guys running around all in black with throwing stars and hiding in shadows…you're not going to find that here. (I was tempted though…and I will have some of <u>those</u> skills taught in another program, I promise.)

What you <u>will</u> find are skills that work so well that people will think you are a *Ninja*, sneaking up on a woman in plain sight and using these super effective skills…with her never knowing what you were doing. *Serious Ninja Skills.* Enjoy.

.

CHAPTER 1- THE ESSENTIALS

Everyone has to start somewhere. The issue right now isn't about where you are starting from and where you think you should be. Focus on where you are now and what you want to accomplish in your life. Start from where you are standing at this moment. This is the best place to start.

"If you cannot find it where you are standing, where do you expect to wander in search of it?"
-Zen

Willing To Learn

Everyone seems to know what they need to do be successful, and yet, how many people are successful? The main component in being successful in any endeavor, especially in the area of communication, is being able to open up your mind and let go of your ego so you can learn.

There is a Zen story about a Journalist from the United States going to Japan to meet with a Zen master. The Journalist was invited to a tea ceremony hosted by the Zen master. The Journalist had done his homework and told about all the things he knew about Zen and the philosophy as the Zen master poured him tea.

As the Journalist continued to go on and on about how much he knew, the Zen master filled the teacup to overflowing and the tea began to spill onto the floor.

The Journalist exclaimed: *"What are you doing? Don't you know that you can't fill the teacup with more tea when it's full?"*

The Zen master replied: *"In order to fill the teacup with more tea, you must first empty it. The mind is like the teacup. If you are wanting to fill the mind, you must first let go of your past assumptions of knowledge and empty your mind."*

If you want to learn more about communication, you might want to *"empty your cup"* and keep an open mind to what I have to share. I can offer you as much information as you can accept, yet until you are willing to learn, the rest will simply overflow and be lost.

Willing To Fail

Have you ever played basketball? How many times have you shot for the hoop and missed? How many times have you actually made it? When you first started out, you missed more often than you made the shot, correct? As you practiced, and shot hundreds, if not thousands of shots, you noticed a pattern.

By learning from your mistakes, you were able to begin to be more consistent in your successes. You began to sink more and more shots. The more that you practiced, the more you were able to be successful with your efforts.

Michael Jordan is known to many of you as one of the greatest basketball players you have ever seen.

Michael wasn't always as good as he was while in the NBA.

When Michael was younger, his brother, Larry, introduced him to the university basketball coach. Michael wanted to join the team and worked hard in order to become a member. The coach had other ideas.

He wanted Michael to be taller. When the time came for the names of the team member picks, Michael read the *"J"* list three times, not seeing his name. He was heartbroken. He admitted that he went home and cried.

His mother saw him and gave him some excellent advice. She told him to work hard and make that coach see that he had made a mistake. This was the turning point for Michael.

Training harder and staying longer than the rest of the team, he became the star of the JV basketball team and began to rise through the ranks into basketball history. This would never have happened had he quit.

Yes, he failed at first; however, he never quit. We all have challenges that come up in our lives. Do we let them get us down, or do we choose to keep working at it until we succeed?

Know What You Want

There is a great book by David P. Campbell called <u>If You Don't Know Where You're Going, You'll Probably End Up Somewhere Else</u>. This small book, only 125 pages, is a great and simple guide to help you figure out what you are wanting in your life.

If we are always looking for what we want in life: money, sex, relationships, happiness, friends, a good job, and more, chances are that we will get some of them.

If we want to get more of them, then we need to be more specific. It is easy to put this into practice. All you have to do is to know what you want and go after it… right? If it were that easy, everyone would be doing it.

Part of being specific is to know what you like first. I found, for myself, that when I was looking for a date, I liked women with a specific body style and hair length.

From there, I looked at her personality and finally her attitudes about life and how she treated others. Seems pretty specific, right? What else was I leaving out?

What I discovered was that body style and hair length were pretty limiting. As I have learned more about myself, I have dated women my height (6') and shorter. Some were plumper, others more thin. Some older than me and most of them younger than me.

Curvy ladies and petite ladies. Short and long hair. Multiple races and hair colors. I discovered that I like women. Not just one type. Yes, I am more attracted to some aspects of women more than others, yet I had to learn what I really wanted in a woman to figure this out. And yes, my specifics have changed as time has passed.

For you to learn what you like, you need to experience meeting and talking and yes, dating, as many women as possible. There are a number of skills involved in this. We will cover many of these skills as we progress through this book.

What Is Your Goal

I've found that when I don't know what I want…I don't get what I want. This principle is very common in our everyday lives. How often have you told yourself that you want a job and pretty soon you get a job…and then find out that you don't like the job?

You then work it as long as you can stand before quitting or finding another job, then quitting your old one, and work the new job only to discover after a few weeks or months that it isn't what you wanted either. Does this sound familiar?

If it does…you're not alone. There is a great saying that I heard from an acquaintance in the past:

"It's better to shoot for the stars and hit the moon than aim for the gutter and hit it."

This saying has served me well over the years to set my sights higher than I normally would have for my goals.

As I have gotten older and wiser, I realize that life is too short to settle for less than what is best for me.

In order to figure out what is best for me, I have to know what I am wanting. My recommendation for your goals is to not focus on the woman that you are wanting, even though that would be a natural thing to work towards.

Instead, focus your goals on being the man that your *"perfect"* woman would want to be with. This is a bit different than you were expecting, isn't it? It is easy to ask someone else to be that *"perfect"* person for you. How often do we expect this of ourselves?

Make your goals the ones that help you to improve your life in a variety of areas. Be a man who has value that grows with the passing of seasons and years, rather than one who expects others to grow their value to suit him.

Demand Your Best

How often have you found yourself saying that this is good enough or close enough or better than nothing?

How often have you accepted where you are in life and allowed yourself to stay comfortable and stagnant in your behaviors and skillsets, rather than expend the effort to improve your own worth or your skills and abilities?

There is nothing sexier to a woman than a man who is confident. Ask any woman. You will find out that women love confidence. Well...how do you develop confidence?

This is one of the easiest questions for me to answer. You develop confidence by being good at something. I mean, really good. Good enough that you can teach someone else how to do that same something.

I love learning skills that improve my value as a man. I have taken the time to learn a variety of skills. Women find men that have skills to be very sexy as well. Cooking...women *love* a man who can cook, and cook well. I am a good cook. Cleaning...yep, you guessed it...women *love* this too.

I can wash dishes and clean my house. I can wash and iron all of my own clothes as well. I love sharp knives when I cook, so I also sharpen all of my own knives (really...how many of you can do this with hair shaving skill?) I can build a campfire for cooking an entire meal or only roast marshmallows.

I can saddle a horse and ride it all day. Unsaddle it and curry it. Set up a campsite complete with tent and fire pit. I can butcher a chicken, rabbit, turkey, deer or squirrel.

I can accurately shoot pistols, rifles and shotguns. I can accurately throw knives and tomahawks while moving. I can hold my breath for two minutes and can swim under and on top of the water. These are a few of the things that I have learned. There are many more.

This is not bragging. It is a statement of fact. What I am doing is explaining to you that I have skills. Skills that give me value in a variety of situations.

I am confident in my abilities and my ability to handle a variety of situations when they arise. This is what builds confidence. This is why it is easy for me to have confidence in myself.

I know that I have value. I know I am valuable. It shows in how I move and how I carry myself. These are all things that you can learn to do as well. Most, if not all of the things above can be studied on YouTube. (I learned these skills the old fashioned way…in person and by experience.)

All you have to do is then practice the skills until you are proficient. Now, you can have more confidence. Now, you can do more and be more. You have more value. Be awesome!!!

Keep Trying vs. Keep Doing

My brother-in-law Tim would often say to me *"Even a steer can try"* when people would say *"I'll try."* For those of you who don't know what a *steer* is, it is a castrated bull (yes, the bull's balls were cut off).

A bull can *"try"* and a cow will get pregnant. A steer can try all day and it won't get anything productive done. So…in your life…are you *"doing"* or *"trying"*?

Master Yoda is one of my heroes. Yes, he is a two foot tall wrinkly green dude who speaks weird, yet he is still one of my heroes.

"Do or do not...there is no try."

His phrase is one of my favorites. I have been using it for the past couple of decades, and it never gets old. The reason it stays fresh is because of the truth in the statement.

Are we always trying? When we try...are we really accomplishing anything? Or are we simply making the motions and willing to back off and falter when it gets a bit tough?

If we really want to accomplish anything in our lives, we shouldn't try. We should do. By *doing* we will create the mental strength and toughness that will support us when things get hard.

It will help us to push forward when it is no longer easy. Just because it is difficult doesn't mean we are unable to do it. It means that through our efforts we will accomplish our desires.

It means that we can progress and move forward in our goals and dreams if only we keep doing. Stop trying. Do. Keep doing. Keep creating your life by your work and ***"do-ings."***

CHAPTER 2 – FIRST STEPS

The journey of a thousand miles begins with a single step. In life, it's way too easy to blame others for where we are or where we've been and the hardships we have had to endure because of their choices. When do we choose to take responsibility for our life? When do we choose to make that decision? We can't change anyone else. We need to start with our self.

Start With You

It is really easy to point the finger at other people for what they are doing or not doing. Seeing their imperfections is the easiest thing in the world to do. What isn't as easy is looking for those imperfections within our self. I know I'm not perfect. I am made well aware of this on a daily basis. Even though I'm not perfect (give me two weeks…maybe then!), I'm still willing to objectively look at myself and discover where I can improve.

Mahatma Gandhi said:

> *"We must become the change we want to see in the world."*

This is a principle that I have made a part of my daily life. I realize that if I don't change, how can I expect anyone else to change? And if I make the effort to change, I will be making the difference to create my world on my terms. We are the beginning from where change starts.

You may be asking yourself:

"Well...why should I change? I'm happy with the person I am right now. I am good enough the way I am and shouldn't have to change."

If you are thinking this way, please put down this book and don't read any more. It will challenge that thinking pattern that you are *"good enough as you are and shouldn't have to change"* -- and that wouldn't be comfortable for you.

The only thing in this world that is constant is change. You can choose to change in a positive way or you can choose to change in a negative way.

You won't get away from it no matter how hard you try.

If you don't eat enough food, you will change. If you eat too much food, you will change. If you exercise, you will change. If you don't exercise, you will change. If you choose to breathe, you will change. If you choose to not breathe, you will notice a change...radically and quite quickly.

Life is about change. If you want to change your life *(reading this book tells me that you are interested in this...even if it's just a little)* then you had best start with yourself. If you don't make the effort to change how you are, no one else will take the effort either.

What Makes You Different?

We all have physical differences. Long hair, short hair, bald, balding or shaved head. Tall, short, fat, skinny, muscular or lean.

The physical differences we have don't make us who we are. They are simply a way for people to recognize us when they see us or meet us in their daily lives. We are more than the way we look.

Take a quick look inside yourself and be honest with yourself… What do you see? Who are you as a person? What have you done to separate yourself from your friends? Siblings? Co-workers?

Knowing who you are and what makes you different is what allows you to be recognized for the person you are, not simply another faceless person in the crowd.

I am a lifetime member of an entrepreneurial organization by the name of *CEO Space International*.

They work with small business owners and entrepreneurs around the world. When I went to my first *Forum*, a week-long tradeshow event held five times a year, one of the questions I was asked was:

"What makes you different from your competitors?"

That was simple enough and I had an answer in my mind:

"The crisis intervention and de-escalation skills I teach, along with the verbal and non-verbal communication skills are fantastic, and some of the best in my industry.

Yet what really sets me apart from my competitors, was my physical control and restraint skills and training.

No other company in the entire troubled youth industry has anything that even comes close to these skills. The level of expertise that I have, combined, with the communication material I teach, sets me apart from my competitors."

Once I shared this with my mentors at *CEO Space*, we then had something that we could work with. What makes <u>you</u> different? Write it down right now.

Take the time to do this exercise. I'm serious. Get out a sheet of paper and write it or type it out. It will show <u>you</u> that you are different, and that's a good thing. It sets you apart from your competition. It not only shows others how different you are, it also reminds you how great you are.

What Makes You Great?

Ok, we know what makes you different, right? You took the time to write down the many things that set you apart from others, right? Your childhood, your siblings or lack thereof, your position at your job or business, your friends, your skills and abilities.

You wrote them all down, right? If not, do it now. You will be surprised at how many things you have, know, or do that set you apart from other people.

Now that you know how you are different, you can now begin to examine your list for what makes you great. Now, you may be asking yourself:

*"What does this have to do with **Ninja Daitng Skills**?"*

An excellent question. And I'll tell you the answer. What this has to do with *Ninja Dating Skills* is this: <u>*If you don't know who you are, why you are interesting or why*</u>

you are a better catch than another man, then neither will she.

By examining the things that set you apart from the rest of the men out there, you become an individual. Someone who is different and unique.

You are someone accomplished in your own areas of expertise and in your life. These things, though to you may not seem very interesting or noteworthy, to the right woman these will be areas and subjects of interest that help to build a deeper relationship. That is why you need to know what makes you great.

When you know what makes you great and why you are so awesome, it shows. It shows in how you walk, talk and interact with the world around you. It also shows when you don't know who you are.

This is why we are focusing on improving you from the inside out. It starts inside your own mind.

Make another list now that details what makes you great. I'm serious, make that list right now. Knowing yourself is how you progress on your journey to greatness. To paraphrase an ancient Greek saying: _"Know yourself."_

What Are Your Assets?

When you think of assets, what are they? Gold? Silver? Piles of currency? A nice car or home? Are these assets? Well, yes they are...however; they aren't the assets we are looking for at this time.

These things are great, and help you to be secure in the long term, yet right now I am thinking: What are your _"internal"_ assets?

Internal assets are those skills, abilities, paradigms, philosophies, and anything else that allows you to be someone who adds value to the lives of others.

"Value to the lives of others?" you may say. *"Yes!"* I reply. **Think about it!**

When you have something of *value*, in whose mind does that value exist? When you believe you are the most perfect specimen of humanity that ever existed, is this belief shared with the greater world at large? If so, you are so much further ahead of the rest of us that you should write a book about your greatness. I'd read it!

If you and your tremendous *value* aren't recognized by the people around you and the world, then what is your *value*, truly?

It is through the eyes and in the minds of others that *value* is established. By your having <u>internal</u> assets that are valuable to others, your <u>external</u> *value* has now gone up.

By increasing the availability to others of your internal assets, your external value will increase. This shows when you receive a raise.

Your employer has seen more of your internal assets and rewards you accordingly. It's also why you don't get a raise. Your internal assets aren't visible to your employer.

This directly applies to the dating world. When you have value that is recognized in the eyes of others, your value improves in the eyes of the women you want to date.

They will see you more as you see yourself when your value is greater. When you don't show that value to the world, then the women also see and recognize that.

Women are great "talent scouts." They see into your heart and soul when it comes to value. Many of them will see the greatness within you and are willing to be patient and be with you as it continues to come forth. Other women want to have that value visible right now.

When you recognize this value and bring it out, you will begin to recognize that people, yes, that includes women, will look at you differently. They will see your internal value showing in how you walk, talk, and your body language. Welcome to the world of value. I knew you had it in you.

How Do You Want To Be?

There is only one person that can change you, and that is <u>YOU</u>! No one else can change you without your permission. The interesting thing is that you have two parts of your mind, your subconscious and your conscious mind.

The conscious mind controls the things you focus on in the present moment. It also thinks of the future and the past.

The conscious mind, even though it is keeping track of what we are doing right now, really doesn't have much control over our actions. It is our subconscious mind that governs our actions and behaviors.

You might say:

"No way! I am in charge of my life and I can change anytime that I want to."

If you believe that, then – <u>Change already</u>! Go ahead, I dare you. The problem with that is in trying to change, you are mainly using your conscious mind.

28

The conscious mind can only focus on 6-7 things at the same time. The conscious mind allows us to think and reason, and go through the routines of the day and keep us as safe as possible while we're living our lives.

The subconscious mind can keep track of *millions*, *billions* and more actions every moment. Think about it.

Your body, with every organ, gland, muscle, and cell are controlled by the subconscious portion of your mind. Do you really think you can compete with that using your conscious mind? You can't. Not really.

What you can do is you can trick your subcionscious with your <u>conscious</u> mind. Trying to change with just your conscious mind isn't going to work.

Using willpower isn't enough. It takes being able to influence your subconscious mind while using your conscious mind, when your subconscious mind is most susceptible to get the results you want.

Hypnosis influences the subsconcious mind, so does NLP, *Neuro Linguistic Programming*, as well as other mental programming techniques.

For me, I've found one of the easiest (most simple and quick), is to focus for a few minutes on the things I want to change in my life about 15-20 minutes right *after* I get up in the morning and about 15-20 minutes right *before* I go to bed at night.

This is when the filter between the conscious and subconscious is most open to suggestion. By having a list of affirmations or declarations that you want to focus on, as well as a *vision board* (a cork board, poster board, or area on your wall where you have a collage of objects or goals you want and want to focus on) you can begin the process of re-training or re-programming your subconscious mind.

You are able to connect to both the left and right sides of your brain, by looking at and thinking about your goals.

It's like programming your subconscious with the right *software* that figures out how to achieve goals and keeps you committed to keep working on your goals until they are achieved. If you don't update your *software* you will keep using your old programming that isn't working for you.

This re-programming helps your conscious mind and your *desires/goals* to sneak past the mental filter that protects the subconscious mind from the daily flood of information that your consciuous mind processes. This filter is called the *reticular activation system, or RAS*.

When you get past the *RAS* and introduce your subconscious mind to these new *goals/desires* and new programming, it can turn this new information into programs that will change your behaviors and get you the results you are wanting.

Holding onto old behaviors is something the subconscious mind does very well. The subconscious is running the *software* for all these goals and behaviors constantly. Some of these behaviors aren't as effective as you might want them to be. Look at your life and where you are right now.

Your life is the direct result of your behaviors. To change can be hard, we've all experienced this, yet it is possible when we have the proper motivation. When we have the motivation, we can create new behaviors that the subconscious will recognize and begin running <u>those</u> new programs to achieve our goals.

By choosing what you want to focus on and have as a behavior, you can change how you are acting and what you are doing in your life. This will help change you into the person you want to be.

Focus On Your Vision

As I mentioned above, it is important to get your subconscious mind involved and to work with you as if you are both on the same team. If you treat your subconscious as something alien and wild, untamable and impossible to change, you will be right.

Henry Ford said:

"Whether you think you can, or think you can't— you're right."

This means that the first step is to believe that you can succeed. By understanding your mind, you can take advantage of how it works and exploit these quirks to help you and your mind work together to be successful.

One of the things I have learned to make this partnership between our conscious and subconscious minds work well, is to have both verbal or written words as well as pictures to speak to the left and right hemispheres of our brain.

This combination of words <u>and</u> pictures speaks volumes to our subconscious mind and the more that we look at these pictures and statements, the more they become imbedded in our subconscious.

Earlier, I mentioned a *vision board*. They are easy to make and to use. The way to use a vision board is:

Get a board or even an area on your wall. Outline it with tape if it is on your wall (I use the Frog tape in the painting supply area at hardware stores. Paint works too if you are wanting to make it permanent) and then place the pictures of things you want to have or accomplish along with the written statements that tell your subconscious mind what you want to have or accomplish.

Have things that you want or want to accomplish that vary in difficulty. This helps the conscious mind to accept that these things are possible to achieve quickly...even if just a few of them. By using both the conscious and subconscious mind together you can change your reality.

Focus on these pictures and written statements right after awaking in the morning and right before bed in the evening.

Keep focused on achieving the goals set out on your *vision board* and expect that you will be successful. Stick with it and you will begin to see the changes happen.

Sounds simple, right? Simple, yes. Effective, yes. Just try it for a month and watch the changes come. Remember: ***It doesn't work if you don't do it!***

I have been using this technique for years and am still amazed at the effectiveness of the *vision board* technique and how, through seemingly small changes, I have been able to consistently change my behaviors and life for the better. Try it. Don't take my word for it. Experience it yourself. You'll be glad you did.

CHAPTER 3 – INSIDE YOUR HEAD

Are you good enough to be with a beautiful woman? Are you smart enough, funny enough, talented enough to attract a woman who is beautiful, talented and loving?

Until you can answer yourself in a positive way and truly accept that you are good enough, the results won't be there. There are things you can do that will help you get to a better place inside of yourself.

Working on you, from the inside out, is the way to change the world. Your world. You <u>are</u> worth it. You deserve it.

Self-Talk

Have you ever listened to the conversations going on in your head? I know, you don't want to admit that you talk to yourself, or that you hear *"voices"*, or you talk to yourself <u>and</u> hear *"voices"* at the same time, and yet it is completely normal.

We all have an internal dialogue going on in our heads. We talk out problems or ask questions hoping for answers. We argue with our parents in the past or friends in the present, and often times, when things didn't go as well for us in a past confrontation, we will replay it and tell ourselves *"Yeah, I should've said that!"*

Having these types of internal conversations is not a bad thing. It isn't a good thing. It is simply a thing. It is a tool that helps you to work through the experiences you have in your life. How do you choose to use this *"Internal Conversation System"* that you have installed in your mind?

One of the most common things that this *Internal Conversation System*, or *ICS* does is to give you a way to communicate with yourself. Believe it or not, your mind listens to every word that you speak, both internally as well as externally. Interestingly enough, the words you speak out loud are actually more impactful than the words that you speak internally.

> *"The more that you say one type of thing, the more you will believe it. Good or bad. Positive or negative."*

The problem with that saying is that it is absolutely true. That's also why it's so awesome. Changing the way that you talk to yourself can change your life.

When I first heard about this *"self-talk"* stuff, it was in the early 1990's. There was this guy, Anthony Robbins, who had a cassette course called *"Personal Power"* that lasted for 30 days. It was supposed to help you on your road to success.

I listened to the cassettes religiously, and one of the topics he spoke about was our internal dialogue that we have with ourselves.

He taught that: *what we talk about and think about, we bring about into our lives. If we constantly had self-talk about how hard our life was or how school sucked or how stupid people were...we'd begin to believe these things.*

He then went on to explain that when we have positive thoughts and words to say to ourselves, we also begin to change our beliefs and thoughts.

He taught me that I can use my brain for thinking about how I can get through my life challenges. Thinking about how I <u>CAN</u> handle my life problems. Thinking about how I can make my life better and how to make the changes I need to get there.

Anthony Robbins was one of the people instrumental in inspiring me to change my life at that young age.

He helped me to recognize that I was in charge of my thoughts. Because of this, I was in charge of my life. What is your self-talk like?

Breathe and Count

The Chinese have a name for when your mind is on overload and chattering at you from a thousand different directions. They call this *"The Monkey Mind."* A very good description. I have had the issue of *"Shiny!!!"* and *"Squirrels!!!"* and am easily distracted when I am not focused on a project. Is this an issue for you too?

Because I am a bit high energy when I am excited about something, a friend in the past called me *"a hummingbird-on-crack."*

I found that I would speak a bit more rapidly than most people could easily follow. I would speak too fast and my brain would jump from topic to topic with no apparent sense of logic or reason…beyond that of my own mind of course. There had to be a way to begin to *"rein in"* on this…issue.

Remember the above section on *Self-Talk*. Think it's hard and it is. Think it's not and…it isn't. (well…not as much anyway.)

I found there was a way to make things easier. There is this handy-dandy little thing called *"meditation."*

I know, I know, meditation is *"sitting with your legs bent into pretzels for hours while you chant and ring bells"*. Right? Wrong.

The Zen practitioners of Buddhism have had this neat little method for teaching beginners and experts alike how to quickly quiet the *Monkey Mind* and to calm it to a level where you can use it to control your mind rather than your mind controlling you.

The name of the technique that I have used for many years I call *"Breathe and Count."*

It is simplicity itself:

First, *sit down in a place where you won't be disturbed for a few minutes.*

Next, *is to take a deep relaxing breath in and let it out calmly saying out loud "one" as you exhale. Then, take another deep relaxing breath in and let it out calmly saying out loud "two" as you exhale. Take another deep relaxing breath in and let it out calmly saying out loud "three" as you exhale.*

Continue *to take deep relaxing breaths in and let them out calmly counting out loud until you reach ten. When you reach ten, repeat the process again, going to ten. Repeat this process of Breathe and Count until you feel calm and relaxed and focused.*

I use this as a quick meditation to get me focused on my work or when I am feeling a bit "anxious" and irritated.

When the *Monkey Mind* has caught me, I have found that this will clear it up in around three *Breathe and Count* cycles of ten. Remember: <u>If you don't use it, it won't work!</u>

Scenario Drills

Have you ever imagined confronting someone who had bullied you? Come on! Yes, you have! I did that plenty when I was younger. Did it help? I don't know if it helped with the bullies, yet it did help with other things in my life.

I have studied martial arts for over 25 years. In that time I discovered that most martial arts used *forms* or *katas* to teach the basic movements of the art.

The *form* or *kata* is a memorized series of movements that simulate interaction with an imaginary opponent. As I progressed in my martial training in my chosen system, I was introduced to *scenario drills*.

These drills simulated, in a much more realistic manner, dealing with multiple attackers in a pre-agreed upon manner, yet working with live bodies.

What this means is if we are working with escaping from a *rear naked choke* hold from behind, I would have someone put the choke on me as other people would attack me slowly, punches or kicks or with knives, batons, baseball bats, etc. I knew the objective, to escape from the choke and stop my opponents without being damaged if possible.

I had trained first with a single opponent (slowly), and then added attackers as I gained the skill to handle them, speeding up as I gained more skill. How I could take care of them was up to me. I had been trained. I knew what to do. Now I needed to *apply* it.

The results were gratifying. Once you train with this method consistently, your speed and skill will increase as your body and mind respond to attackers that you didn't even see coming. It is so cool!!!

"What does this have to do with dating", you might be asking? I'm glad you are asking questions.

How often do you see a woman that you are interested in or want to meet? When you see her, what do you do? How do you react? Do you approach her? Do you talk to her? What do you say?

All of these things come into your mind with a flood. Too much information. Too much input. Too much sensory overload. This is what I experienced when I first started getting back into dating after being married for 15 years and then getting divorced. I didn't know where to start.

I remembered this *scenario drill* idea where we trained simple and slow at first and then increased the difficulty and speed as we progressed. I didn't start out being choked and attacked by three guys with knives at the same time. I started first with being able to get out of a simple choke hold.

This is how you can start your own scenario drills. First decide what would be equivalent to a *choke hold* in the dating world. Pick something that has happened and is commonly encountered while wanting to meet or talk to a woman, such as standing in line at the store and making small talk with a woman, introducing yourself to a woman while at a party, seeing a woman that you have seen before with some friends, and going over to renew your acquaintance.

There are thousands of these types of scenarios we can cover. I prefer to cover general types of scenarios rather than trying to cover all of them. By training for general scenarios we gain skills to adapt and respond to different or unusual scenarios.

What is an easy and inexpensive way to practice? You practice in front of a mirror.

Practice In Front of a Mirror

Training yourself with scenario drills is a great way to get some *"practice"* in talking to women and meeting them for the first time and even reacquainting yourself if you haven't seen her for some time. There is a great book called _Psychocybernetics_ by Maxwell Maltz. Dr. Maltz was a plastic surgeon in the 1940's and 1950's.

What Dr. Maltz realized was that people could have their face changed on the outside with surgery, yet if they didn't change on the inside it didn't matter how much changed on the outside.

He mentions in his book that the nervous system can't tell the difference between a real event and one vividly imagined. The interesting thing is that the subconscious mind can't tell the difference from a real event and one vividly imagined <u>either</u>. That is the key right there.

When you vividly imagine something, your subconscious mind can't tell the difference from a real event or the one you just made up in your mind.

The reason that this is such a powerful concept is that you don't have to be in front of a beautiful woman, attempting to chat her up, and screw up badly twenty times before you are able to do it with any amount of competency.

You can do that in front of your own mirror! Why do I say you will screw up badly twenty times? Because all of us, when learning a new skill, will screw up. I don't look at it as negative. I look at it as learning or training.

You learn by screwing up and figuring out what you did wrong and not doing the *wrong* thing next time. How often did you fall down when you were a baby learning to walk? Way too many times. Did you keep on going? Yes…if you are walking today, the answer is yes.

Using the mirror is the easiest way I've found to practice looking at my body language and how I am smiling and presenting myself to someone.

By introducing myself to the mirror, I can watch to see if I look creepy, bored, interested or, coming across as too much of a *"fanboy"*.

However you have acted or looked like in the past, you were the one that created the negative reaction from the ladies. I've done it. You've done it. We all have.

Let's learn from it now. Imagine standing in line at the store to checkout your groceries. You see an attractive lady behind you with no wedding ring on (or since this is practice, let her have a wedding ring on. I've found married ladies are often easier to talk to because she is already in a relationship.)

Look over your shoulder, turning your body slightly towards her, greet her. (*"Hi"*, *"Hello"*, *"Whoa! Have you tried the other brand on those cheese sticks? Are they any better?"* whatever! Interact!) What does she do? How does she respond?

Our mind is incredible. When we imagine a scenario, our mind comes up with parts for all the players to play. Go through the scenario and watch for hints that you are comfortable or are not comfortable.

This is why you are practicing in front of the mirror. Practice your greeting or conversation twenty (20) times. Yes, do it twenty times. The reason for this is that the subconscious mind has what I call a *"library"* of information always available to it.

When we are remembering an experience, our mind goes and checks the *library*. When it finds nothing, it improvises, and creates a memory to put in that space to refer to the next time it has something like that happening.

When you imagine the experience, and go through it a few times, these become memories in the *library* that your mind will go to and reference when needed. You create the reference.

You create the memories of being able to talk to a woman or ask her to dance or out on a date. All of these are very important in creating the outcome you want.

Calm Mind, Calm Body

How often have you been called on at work or in school or in a social environment to do something uncomfortable? If you are like most humans, this has happened at least a few times in your life.

Did you rise to the challenge of doing that uncomfortable thing? Or did you refuse and lose that opportunity? In the moment you were asked, did you feel anything?

Did you notice a feeling of panic or anxiety? Did you feel yourself starting to sweat or feel any physical discomfort?

Remember the book I mentioned, *Psychocybernetics* by Maxwell Maltz? In the book, he mentions how the body is controlled by the brain. He also mentioned that we have within our mind what he calls the *"Automatic Success Mechanism."* This *Automatic Success Mechanism*, or *ASM* as we will call it, is a part of our mind that will complete tasks that we've programmed the *ASM* to do. It is our mind that programs the *ASM*.

When we program it to be successful and to accomplish that 2 mile run after work, it does it. If it is programed to stutter and blush when a woman comes up to you and asks your name, it also accomplishes that. The *ASM* does whatever it has been programmed to do. It does not judge the programming as good or bad. It simply is a program to be executed.

The *ASM* can be used to benefit us in our lives and in the pursuit of our goals. One goal of mine has been to be calm and confident in stressful situations.

Having been in the military, as well as owning my own business and giving presentations and trainings to professionals, I've found that as I had my mind calm, my body followed.

I have realized that as I was confident in presenting my material for the training, my mind was calm. When my mind was calm, my body followed in being calm as well.

My presentations are always better when my mind is calm. I interact with the participants more smoothly and my answers to questions, even ones that I don't know the answer to, are more applicable and appropriate to the situation when my mind is calm.

You are in control of your mind and your body. Remember that in order to calm your body, you must calm your mind first.

Change Your Body, Change Your Mind

There was a song that came out back in 2000 by the music group *Sister Hazel* called <u>Change Your Mind</u>. The lyrics went: *If you want to be somebody else, change your mind.* When I first heard that, I thought they were telling me <u>not</u> to want to be somebody else.

I thought they were saying that it <u>wasn't</u> a good thing to try and be someone else, instead to be happy being me. The lyrics do follow that message of being happy by being myself. However…what I realized, since I had read and listened to many books on self-help and self-improvement by that time, that another meaning was also buried within those lyrics.

If you want to be somebody else, change your mind. If you want to be someone different than you are right now, if you want to be more than you are right now, change your mind.

If you want to be a different person, a better person, than you are today, there is only one thing that will cause that to happen. <u>Change your mind</u>.

You can change how you think. You can change how you act. You can change the programming in your mind.

Because of this revelation about the lyrics for this song, I realized that all of the self-help and improvement books and audios I had been learning from for the past few years had been condensed down to a few simple thoughts:

You are in charge of your own destiny. You can change it through changing your mind.
The answers that you are looking for <u>are</u> inside of you.
You don't need someone else to tell you what to do every step of the way.
Ask yourself and the answers will be there.

Wow! What a concept! Armed with this information, I realized that I was good enough, <u>and</u> smart enough to become the person that I wanted to be. I wasn't there yet, though I had a direction now and the *idea* of where I wanted to be. From that <u>*idea*</u>, I began to change who I was and how I thought.

It was still a rough road, no doubt about it. My life still wasn't going entirely the way that I wanted, yet it was changing as I changed my mind.

I then discovered more information in my studies and research into human potential, which is the name the whole *"self-help and self-improvement"* industry was stepping into.

Your mind has the ability to change your body. Not just on the external level. It has the ability to change your immune system and how your body functions. The area of study is called *psychoneuroimmunology*.

We have the ability to influence our body with the quality of our thoughts. By changing how we think, we can change the behaviors we have for health and wellness.

By changing our behaviors for health and wellness, we have changed our bodies. The only thing constant in this life is change.

Which direction do you want to change? That's up to you.

CHAPTER 4 – MORE THAN WORDS

They say that a picture is worth a thousand words. So, what is a movie then? Hundreds of thousands of words? Millions of words?

Everywhere we go, and everything we do is being seen by people around us, and I'm not just talking about the creepy security cameras that seem to be everywhere.

I'm talking about your body language and what it is constantly communicating to the world. Do you realize what you are *"saying"* to the world?

It's Not What You Say; It's How You Say It

Ever heard the phrase *"Actions speak louder than words?"* If you have, great. If you haven't, you're hearing it now. This is a tremendously valuable saying to remember and even to memorize when it comes to communication.

Everything we say and do is communicating to the world around us. Everything that is said and done around us from the world is communicating to us. The cycle is never ending. However, even though there is such a flood of information coming to us from the world, there are ways to use this information for our benefit.

Realize this: most of us have two eyes, two ears, a nose, two hands and a mouth. Our skin feels sensations and our feet carry us around in a relatively efficient means to get through our lives. Our senses are what I am talking about. We see. We hear. We smell. We taste. We feel with our hands and our skin.

We move our body in place and from one place to another. Just because you may not have some of these senses, rest assured, the information that even some of these body parts can offer are more than enough to better understand the interaction between humans and the rest of the world. For those of you who might be wondering, yes, women (females) are in that *"human"* category.

All of this ties into the statement, *"It's not what you say; it's how you say it."* As I was growing up, I was often chastised by my mother to *"speak nicer to your sisters,"* or, *"you don't have to like that person, you just have to be nice to them,"* or *"don't look at me like that,"* or *"I don't like the tone of your voice."*

Do these sound familiar? I have lived through every one of these multiple times. I think we all have. The thing is, it seems that what we were being taught to do was to lie convincingly to others, not to communicate in a better manner.

We were told to do one thing, *be nice*, and not to work with or understand the emotions of anger or frustration, behind the actions. It seems we've been taught to make our feelings and our actions be opposite to how we act and communicate.

Yes, your body language changes when your feelings change. When our feelings and our actions aren't the communicating the same message, it's called *"being out of congruence."*

When we are *"out of congruence,"* our words don't match the actions and message being communicated to our audience. Think of a greasy shyster used car salesman. His words (*"trust me"*) and his actions (*"I'm going to cheat you and get away with it"*) send a conflicting message to you.

As I grew older and as I learned to study about how our communication and body language fit together, a whole new world opened up to me. I learned that *"All Behavior is Communication."*

Body Language 101

As I said in the previous section, *"All Behavior is Communication."* Think about it. Every breath that you take. Every eye motion you make. Every twitch of your finger, nose, eyebrow, mouth, knee, or foot is communicating to people around you. Yes, each one of those does mean something to the people that can decypher that information.

Additionally, there are other things that add to the mix when you throw in how you use your voice, and how close or far you are from the person. That's even before the person pays attention to the words coming out of your mouth.

I know you will be familiar with some of the basics of *Body Language* that I am bringing up here, so be patient with me. Some of the other information given off through *Body Language* you might not have recognized for their importance. All in all, this is just the tip of a very big iceberg.

Body language in its most basic sense consists of:

Eye contact and motions: Yes, looking someone in the eye is considered body language. It is tremendously important to being able to make a connection with someone and build a feeling of trust.

Realize that different cultures have different ideas of what is acceptable in eye contact. For now, we are dealing with what is acceptable in North America, in general.

Gestures: Hand gestures, shoulder shrugs, one finger waves (yes, I mean flipping the bird), and other gestures with your hips, feet, head cocked to one side, hands on your hips, rocking back and forth. You get the idea. There are a bunch.

Facial expressions: Smiles, smirks, eyebrow raises, grimace, snarl, disgust, surprise and many more. You've seen them. These are body language and each one has a meaning that tells you more of the story than just the words the person says.

Body movements and positioning: I find these crucial for building any kind of trust as I interact with people and most especially when I am meeting and dating a woman.

When you face a woman too directly, and squarely with your torso facing her, think of your torso as a powerful spotlight…the strong intensity isn't comfortable shining right at her. When you first meet her, this can be intimidating and too intense.

Showing too much attraction too soon is creepy. Shifting your body to other positions can change how people feel about you and how you are perceived.

Physical contact: There are specific zones that are pretty universal in what is appropriate to touch when you have first met a person and how those zones change as you build the relationship.

Also, how much and for how long you touch these areas are important to be aware of.

Breathing patterns: As strange as it sounds, understanding the breathing patterns of a person can tell you quite a bit about their emotional state. Slow even breathing, when they are conscious, can mean they are relaxed and present; shallow and quiet can mean they are focused, maybe reading; short fast breaths can mean excited or frightened.

All of these are subject to what is happening to the person when you are watching for the clues to how they are feeling and acting.

Distancing and the Bubble

Distancing is more than simply how close you are to a person. It equally equates to how far you are from a person.

Understanding that distancing ties in with body language, most especially with body movements and positioning, helps this information to make more sense. Recognize that everyone has their own concept of personal space.

What is personal space? Personal space is the zone around your body where you feel most at ease when you are around other people. This is usually an arm's length away from your torso. It is far enough away from you for you to feel comfortable, yet it gives you the room you need to interact with others without alienating them. When people invade your space, your comfort goes down and you instinctively will want to create that distance again to feel comfortable.

It is also the space that you allow someone you trust to enter into and be close to your body. When you trust people and enjoy their company (yes, women apply here…or men, depending on your preference), your space then blends with theirs. The culture in which you were raised can influence the area of your personal space preference. Social or business settings can also influence what is accepted or comfortable.

One of the easiest ways to explain this is by thinking about the space around you as a *bubble*. Put your arms out to your sides with your fingers extended: at the top of your fingers is the edge of your *bubble* of personal space.

Put your arms out in front of you fingers extended forward. This is also the edge of your *bubble*. It is, as a general rule, an arm's length in front of you and to your sides and in back of you.

When people approach you, as well as when you approach someone else, they have a *bubble* that travels with them.

When their *bubble* and yours come into contact, you have found the comfortable distance to communicate and converse with a stranger. Everyone's *bubbles* are different sizes. If you are too close to a stranger they will back up. Or, depending on the culture, they may be right up in your face because that is what they feel comfortable with. If you're not sure how close to be, start farther away and <u>then</u> close the gap gradually to show interest and respect instead of a threat.

The concept of the *"bubble"* isn't new, and yet so many men I know haven't really learned how to use the *bubble* to their advantage. In fact, they use it like a blunt instrument to attack a woman's *bubble* and force their attention and sometimes affection on her. Not cool, bro. Not cool.

There are much better ways to do this. Using your *bubble* to push into hers is the fastest way to being rejected.

By not respecting her space, and attempting to force your attention on a woman, you are intruding into her space and that could be viewed as a form of assault.

We'll talk more about the *bubble* in a bit.

Voice Tones

Has someone ever complimented you and you took it as an insult? I know I have. I've had siblings, kids from school, and drill sergeants in the *United States Army* all compliment me…in tones that told me that they were feeling very different than the words that they had just spoken to me. Yes, sarcasm is in this same category.

Learning to control our body is pretty natural to us. It was something that we have been taught since we were young.

As time passed, we also learned to control our voice in ways that helped us to get what we wanted. Hey…it's true! We learned to manipulate with our voice at a very young age. As newborn babies to be exact. We are hungry…<u>WHAAAAAAA!</u> We want to get our diaper changed…<u>WHAAAAAAA!</u> We are tired and want to go to sleep…<u>WHAAAAAAA!</u> Get the picture?

Just because we want something, doesn't mean we should cry to get it. That doesn't work as well when you get older. Some people, though, have learned that when they cried in the past (think about a woman who cries to get out of a speeding ticket), they were rewarded by getting their way.

A word of advice guys, don't *whine* or *cry* to get affection or attention from a woman. It gives off a very negative message that women <u>DO NOT</u> find attractive.

I'm not talking about showing emotion. What I'm talking about is *whining, crying,* or *begging* for their attention and affection. Honest emotions are respected and valued.

<u>Here are some other aspects of voice tones that I want to cover:</u>

Fluency: This deals not only with being *able to* speak in the language you are communicating in, it also deals with *how well* you speak the language you are communicating in.

I know native English speakers who suck at being able to speak in a fluent manner. I have a hard time speaking to them, let alone speaking with a foreigner that doesn't speak English as well.

<u>*When speaking and focusing on fluency*</u>: *make sure you are focusing on the words coming out smoothly and not bunched up or choppy.*

Inflections: This is what often catches our ear when speaking to the used car salesman or the friend who is always saying something that grates on your nerves…even though there was nothing wrong with the words that were said. It was *how* they were said.

The inflections, the small changes to the words in their tones that makes a statement (What!) to a question (What?) to a tease (hmmm…whaaat? A grin is necessary here). Sarcasm relies on inflections to be as effective as they are.

Pauses: Often times when we are listening to someone else, we want to offer insight or ask questions or demonstrate our intellect.

When we are asked a question in a conversation, we often jump immediately in with the answer that is burning to get out…and that demonstrates that we weren't really listening to the other speaker.

Learning to pause when you are asked a question…to give the impression that you are thinking about your response…and then giving the other person your answer, shows an amount of respect to the other person (your date?), that builds the relationship.

If you simply jump into the conversation and don't pay attention to who you steamroll verbally to get your point in, you will be remembered as a rude person with no respect who doesn't have the brains to realize how much they screwed up. (I had a girlfriend once who would do that…needless to say that I wasn't with her long.)

Stuttering: Stuttering is sometimes a part of life. I've had friends who stutter and that is simply a challenge that they have lived with their entire lives.

If you don't normally have this condition in your life, and you still stutter <u>because</u> you don't know what to say or are nervous, recognize that you can improve and possibly fix that. Practicing calming exercises can help you to avoid the nervous-stuttering. (Remember: *Breathe and Count* exercise in **Chapter 3**.)

My friends would be affected more when they were nervous or anxious and sometimes excited. Calm yourself and your breathing. It will help you to have a smoother speaking pattern.

Tempo: Tempo is something like dancing. There is a rhythm to the conversation, a flow. If you don't pay attention to it, you will step on some toes.

Paying attention to the tempo will allow you to move from one conversation and subject to another in a flow.

Realize you don't have to be firing off words like a machine gun or chattering like a *hummingbird-on-crack*!

Slow down your tempo if anything. It will improve your conversations and help the listener to understand what you have to say.

Volume: Unless you are in a hurricane or near a demolition site, or at a rock concert, YOU SHOULDN'T HAVE TO YELL! Paying attention to your volume, both positive and negative, is important.

Being shy and talking to your navel when there is a woman across from you on a date isn't very attractive. Neither is nearly shouting to that same woman across the table from you (spitting often comes with shouting as a byproduct...that should also be avoided). Control your volume to match your environment.

Positive vs. Negative Body Language

When I first heard about *"positive"* and *"negative"* body language, I was confused. I knew that there was body language that could be taken as positive and some that could be thought of as negative, and yet, what made body language *"positive"* or *"negative"*?

Normally, I had learned that body language isn't specifically *positive* or *negative*, it's just information. When you begin to look at body language for dating, *positive* and *negative* take on different meanings.

Having *positive* body language, in essence, is having a body language that is displaying interest or attraction to another person. (Which pretty much is the same thing. *Attraction* is only interest…for now.)

The best part, when you understand it, is that this *positive* and *negative* body language goes both ways. She will also show *positive* body language towards <u>YOU</u> when she is interested.

This would include, and yet not be limited to:

- Turning the torso (chest and belly) towards the other person.
- A complete smile (covered in the next chapter)
- Touching the area of the neck between the collar bones (the little hollow at the base of the throat. It is often touched as a sign of feeling nervous or timid) and neck exposure.
- Touching you (your arm, hand, leg etc. This also includes pushing or punching when it is gentle. If she punches you in the face you shouldn't take it as her liking you, unless she kisses you right after. **<u>A lot!</u>** LOL.)

There are many, many more of these that can be covered at a later time.

Next is the *negative* body language that she will show when she is NOT interested. This would include and yet not be limited to:

- Leaning away from you.
- Turning her torso away from you.
- Negative facial expressions (sneers, scowl, rolling eyes, etc.)
- Grabbing your hand from where you touch her and removing it or intercepting your hand as it reaches out to touch and/or knocking it away.

There are so many more of these that can be added to this list. These are a few common signals that you can avoid when you are aware of them.

Appearance

You'd think that appearance would be a no-brainer, right? Well, you're wrong. Appearance is something that is very important that some guys just don't get, especially as they get older and more comfortable with their lifestyle and mindset.

Paying attention to your appearance will not only make you feel better about yourself, it also shows other people how you feel about yourself as well.

Dress in dirty and rumpled clothing that is wrinkled and smells like last week's gym shorts, guess how people will think you feel about yourself.

Yes, I said *"...guess how people will think you feel about yourself."* How people think of us will have an impact on how we are perceived and thought of by others.

You may be saying to yourself:

"Well, if they don't accept me for how I am, then they aren't the one for me."

That is the attitude of a child. If you are an adult, then start acting like one. Just because your mother said that *"you are awesome"* and *"I love you"* and *"you are good enough just the way you are"* doesn't mean that others will see you the same way.

The world isn't your mom. The world doesn't care. The world is a cold and hard place that has no regard for your feelings or ego. Honestly, get over it. Yes, I am being brutal here. It is for good reason.

Choosing to be out in the world for dating, socializing, or even for going to work, can be a scary thing.

Yes, I said scary. For most guys (I was one of them) having to go out and meet a woman was scarier than public speaking, a vicious dog or a human attacker. (I honestly was more comfortable with a human attacker even a few years ago.)

The reason for this I've found is the *rejection factor*. We men have this primal fear of *rejection*. We don't want to put ourselves in harm's way (from our brain's primitive perspective) and risk being damaged (mostly emotionally…usually not physically).

Being able to make a good first impression is key to being able to get over the first hurdle of *"rejection"*.

We'll cover that more in a later chapter. Needless to say, it is important to choose how you want to be perceived by the world around you.

Develop your personal style. A style that defines you and sets you apart from other men. If you want to go for the bell bottoms and comb overs in a plaid shirt…well, that might work in the right venues, yet for the most part that look will be a warning sign of what to avoid, **you**. Bring your wardrobe up to date, at least in the last decade. It will make a difference.

My personal style is, for the most part, dark blue jeans and a dark, usually black, t-shirt or knit shirt. I prefer black. It is a simple and comfortable color to me. As time has passed, I purchase better quality and more fashionable black t-shirts. Yet black is my mainstay color.

I have a few greys, navy blues and even a few lighter colored shirts, yet black is my go to that matches with my other clothes. People associate me now for my colors, and it's a part of my personality. In the fall and winter, I wear grey, tan or black sweaters over my shirts.

I also often wear a scarf, preferably one that is in good condition (don't machine wash them unless it says so on the tag). They are also of darker colors.

My jackets are all black in a variety of styles. *Columbia* is the main brand I buy for my outerwear. My heavy coat is also *Columbia*. *Columbia* is excellent quality for the money and a well-known outdoor brand.

I also have a leather jacket I wear occasionally. I wear black ball caps in the warmer times of the year and a black knit cap in the winter.

When I am at a business meeting or convention, I wear darker colors. Blues, blacks and greys for my dress shirts. My suits are usually dark charcoal, dark green, or black. These colors go well with my skin tone.

This is my personal style. I am confident in how I look in my clothing. I make sure that they fit me well. I wear my hair short and have a beard that I keep short and well trimmed. I wear glasses and look for eyewear that compliment <u>my</u> <u>personal</u> style. I mostly wear leather shoes, colors are…you guessed it, blacks and greys.

Find a style that works for you. Don't try to dress like a 20-something guy unless you are a 20-something guy. Find an image consultant if you can afford it. If not, do a *Google* search and look on *YouTube* for styles to wear for your age range.

Look online and search for colors, hairstyles, clothing and accessories that you should have in your wardrobe.

Go to stores and try on different styles and looks of clothing. It's okay to ask a salesperson for their suggestions and opinions. Thank them for their opinion and then make your own decisions.

If you have hair, have it cut professionally. Pick a style that makes you feel good and feel confident. (I often tell my stylist to *"Make me sexier than I already am."* It instantly gets a smile and starts a conversation.)

Some guys consider hair color to cover your silver/grey or to change their look; it's okay to enhance your image, yet grey can be sexy. I am proud of my silver hair in both my beard as well as at my temples.

Check out different grooming products. If you don't have hair or are balding, either trim what you have-- no comb overs, or *Bic* it (shave your head!).

Bald is cool and sexy. I know ladies who absolutely love bald guys and don't date any men with hair. Rock your bald head and be proud. Take care of your scalp, with or without hair.

   Remember guys: Ladies like that bit of grey or silver in your hair or beard. It is a sign of age, wisdom and refinement. We men age like fine wine; We get better as we get older. (or…we're supposed to anyway)

Clean and healthy skin is sexy. Acne and pock marks aren't just kid stuff, so check out ways to zap the zits. While you're at it…moisturizer and sunscreen aren't just for ladies and can help you feel smooth and avoid skin cancer (not a good look).

Got facial hair? If you tend to _5-o'clock shadow_ early in the day, consider shaving before a date. Just don't reek of aftershave or cologne. A little goes a long way.
   Is a beard or mustache your deal? If so, a closer trim may help you look younger and more approachable. As for long scraggly eyebrows, nose or ear hairs – trim is in!
   Body hair may be your heritage, but you do have a choice nowadays as to how you accept it. Rock it or remove it – as do the ladies. Everyone has different likes for more or less hair peeking from above or below the collar and/or belt. Groom yourself how you feel comfortable.

Tattoos are a personal art form with a life-time commitment. Piercings, too. Embrace your style. However, accept that some people will enjoy your look more than others. Do the dates you seek like your look as much as you do?
   Overall, remember that the first impression that someone has of you should be your _"best"_ self. We all

have that side of us that doesn't shower or shave for days and wants to sit in front of a fire staring into the dancing flames.

We also have a side that we can bring out that is interested in how we look and how we appear to others, especially women. Be proud of yourself. No one will be proud of you until you are proud of <u>your</u> Self.

CHAPTER 5 – FACE-TO-FACE

In today's fast paced world of electronics and digital communication devices, the skills of meeting and interacting with live people, face-to-face, are becoming something of a lost art. This has become an issue in today's societhy and something I am seeing more and more of in younger generations, and it's getting worse.

The skills of *"interpersonal communication"* aren't being taught in the grade schools or high schools of today. It has becomes an area of academic study once you get into college, more for business instead of dating, where most of your *communication* behaviors are already well established.

You can change this trend. You can be the person who is the *communication* example to others. To do this though, you have to know about and use these *communication* skills yourself.

Eye Contact

Have you ever looked at someone in the eye? I mean really looked them in the eye and noticed the color of their eyes consciously? Have you looked into their eyes and seen your own reflection? Have you ever maintained that eye contact for more than a few heartbeats?

If you haven't done any of these, go out and do each one of these today: *noticing the eye color, seeing your own reflection, and the holding the eye contact.*

I have noticed, both in my own experience as well as hearing from other people and from articles that I have read over the years, that there is less *"eye contact"* in conversations today than there was 20 years ago. I would say that even from 10 years ago there is a significant difference. Why do you think that is?

My answer is *electronic media*. This current generation seems to be losing the ability to effectively communicate *face-to-face* with comfort and skill.

People are so connected to their phones and other devices that talking *face-to-face* with them will usually result in them pulling their phone out to check for messages or to reply to a text at least once or twice during your conversation. Am I right?

Because of this, I wanted to remind you that when you are speaking to someone *face-to-face*, talk to them and look them in the eye, not at your phone.

If you need to answer an important call or text, excuse yourself (*"Excuse me...I need to get this, one moment please"*) and then turn away to take care of the call or text, and then continue with the conversation. Simple manners. They make a big impression.

As for eye contact: Have you ever noticed how people's eyes tend to bounce from one of your eyes to the other or your eyes bouncing from one of their eyes to the other when you are looking at their eyes? DON'T DO

IT!!! This appears that you are looking for something in their eyes and can distract them from what you are saying or distract you from what they are saying.

I will look at the inside corner of one eye. I prefer the left eye, as it ties into the right side of the brain (the right side of the brain deals with creativity and expressing emotions…as well as other things). Using this, I focus (not stare!!!) on the inside edge of their left eye when I speak to people.

My being able to hold eye contact allows me to demonstrate my confidence to the person I am speaking with. Holding eye contact is a great way to show women you are confident.

It can also be a bit intense at times. I will hold my eye contact and break it occasionally and then go right back to the eye contact when I notice that she is looking away from me, as if she is shy.

Watch people today, and from here on out, and notice how many of them will hold eye contact. How many of them will hold it for more than a few seconds? Keep track. The numbers will surprise you.

Holding eye contact is one of the best ways to make a connection with a lady. Talk to her and watch her eyes. Look into her eyes. You will be amazed at how effective this can be.

One Look, Then Focus
When you last spoke to a beautiful woman, where did your eyes go? Did they dwell on her sizable…assets? Or did you look at her face and your eyes kept drifting

downwards…even when you wanted to make a good impression? If your eyes betrayed you, you aren't alone.

Yes, we are men. We visually appreciate the many physical aspects of the feminine body. Front side, as well as backside, and everything in between.

Even though we appreciate the view, realize that staring and losing our focus and concentration to stare at a woman's chest is both impolite *as well as* immature.

Yes, I said immature. *"Why is that"*, you may ask? Are you a boy or a man? Yes, I just answered a question with a question for good reason. By choosing between being a boy or a man, I can then work with you based on your answer.

If you want to be a boy, by all means keep staring at her *boobs* and be lost in her luscious curves. You have to look because chances are you aren't going to get a chance to touch.

Now, if you have chosen to be a man, you need to *"man-up"* and take control of your body and mind.

You have the ability to control a variety of responses that your body has. **You control** where your eyes look and where your hands move. **You control** what you say and where you walk. **You are in control**…when you want to be.

Remember earlier in the book when I mentioned how first impressions are important? If you are so hypnotized by her chest or other body parts, what does this tell her about you?

Are you the man for her when you can't even keep from drooling? **You <u>can</u> control yourself.**

First off, when you see her take one look. **<u>One</u>**. Look her up and down and appreciate what you see (she will notice and appreciate this). Then, focus on her face and the words that she is speaking.

By focusing on her words and not her…other assets, you are demonstrating that she is valued more than just for her looks. This raises your value in her eyes. So remember, One look and then **<u>Focus</u>**!!!

Smiles: Greeting or Warning

A smile is not just a smile. I'm serious. Smiles are a response that is hardwired innto us to greet another when we come into contact with other people.

It is a universal greeting and gesture of friendliness that you will see across the world in human children and adults when they trust you. In animals it has a different meaning.

Animals, when they bare their teeth and especially carnivores, smile as a warning. So, are we humans any different? Do we use the smile as a greeting or as a warning?

The answer is *"yes."* The smile is used as both. So how can we tell which it is? What are the warning signs and how can we tell if a smile is genuine or if it is a *"back-off-and-get-away-you-creeper"* smile?

Well…that depends. I know, that answer isn't what you wanted to hear, and yet, keep reading, and I will explain. The reason that it *"depends"*, is because there are many variables to keep track of to make sure you are getting the proper *"reading"* of the situation.

It sounds complicated, and it is. The more that you pay attention to the *"tells"* or body language hints that are given off, the easier it is to understand what you are looking for. Additionally, the body language hints come in groups called *"Clustering"* that can give you a better idea of the accuracy of the messages you are receiving.

The first area we want to look for is the eyes. When a person is smiling a genuine, full wide grin smile, that smile is reflected in the eyes, causing them to look happy.

There is also a wrinkling of the skin at the edges of the eyes, almost like a slight squint, that happens when the smile is genuine and happy.

If the smile is big around the mouth yet doesn't reach the eyes, which is a good indicator that it is a *"hi-how-are-you-will-you-go-away-now-please"* smile. It is also called the polite smile. Women love it and are very good at using it with each other.

The challenge is that men don't often read the signs well enough to realize that the polite smile isn't meant to get them interested in talking to the woman. It is meant to keep the man away. It is a warning, the same with animals that will bare their teeth.

It is the smile that says *"I-don't-want-to-talk-to-you, yet-I-don't-want-to-appear-too-outwardly-hostile."* It means *"keep-your-distance-please"*.

Another type of common smile is the close lipped smile. The closed lipped smile has a number of varieties; however we will only cover two of those smiles.

One is the personal smile that is usually small and mostly at the corners of the mouth. This personal smile can be an *"I-know-something-you-don't-know"*, or an *"I-don't-want-to-be-here-yet-I-will-smile-and-deal-with-it"* type of smile.

Another, is when the smile is closed lip and yet the smile is larger and wider, like a full grin, yet the lips are pressed closed.

The eyes are usually not happy eyes with the wrinkles at the edges. This smile is usually one of distaste and tolerance, attempting to be nice in a social environment even though something is going on under the surface. Look at prominent politicians and public figures, when they are caught on camera and aren't very happy, for good examples of this.

Remember: Smiles and other *greetings* and *gestures* are simply that: *greetings* and *gestures*. Don't take it personally. They may be having a bad night or have a stomach ache or their feet hurt.

There are so many things to watch for with body language to get a better idea of how someone is feeling and it is easy to misinterpret those signals in the beginning.

Focus on the signals and messages that you do know and recognize and you will get a better idea of what is going on. The other areas can be learned over time.

Remember: Your smile is also seen by others. Practice in front of a mirror. Make sure you are avoiding the things we have discussed here that need to be avoided and focus on the parts that are keys to a better and friendlier smile. Women love men who smile. Practice smiling more.

What to Avoid
You know, I could write another book just on what to avoid when dating. However, I don't want to focus on

what to avoid; I want to focus on the positive things that you can do to improve your dating communication.

The reason that I am having this section is because you also need to know about the things that make it more difficult to build *rapport* (affinity and mutual trust) with a woman. Knowing these *things* and avoiding them are crucial in getting close enough to start that all-important first conversation.

There are a couple of things that I want to focus on in here, because they are huge turn-offs that are immediately recognized by ladies and turn many of them off, or put you in the *"friend zone"* immediately.

First off: brush your teeth. Yes, I said brush (and floss) your teeth. Women recognize the little things that we take time to do to help us be more attractive.

They take the time to do these things to impress us. We should do the same type of things to be more attractive to them.

Having a chunk of broccoli or spinach stuck to your front teeth while talking will absorb her attention, and not in a good way. Also having white gunk all over your teeth because you were too busy to brush your teeth for the past few days also says something to her about your priorities.

A side effect of not brushing your teeth is having bad breath. A HUGE turnoff to women. If you have a medical disorder, teeth problem, or have recently had mouth surgery, your breath can also be horrible.

When I have had dental surgery in the past, my wife (*now ex*) told me I had *"corpse breath."* That hurt my feelings. I still remember how I felt at that time when she jokingly called me *"corpse breath"* and used it afterwards as her personal joke when I had bad breath and how much it emotionally hurt and how angry I got from her words.

However, it did inspire me to take better care of my mouth through keeping it cleaner and fresher. It is a lesson that has stuck with me over a decade later.

<u>Second thing to avoid is</u>: nasty fingernails. Nasty means: long, jagged, chewed, dirty, or in any way *"unhygienic"* nails.

I am a licensed massage therapist in addition to my other businesses, and having good looking nails is a must in this industry. I have never thought that men should have long fingernails for a variety of reasons.

My views are not shared by all people. I once met an African man that had very well taken care of nails that were quite long. He said that among his people the men had longer nails and the women had the shorter nails. Cool. His culture supported that. Ours doesn't.

I often see older men with thick, yellow nails that obviously haven't been cut for the past month or six. If you want to impress women, don't be one of those men.

Having dirt, grease or anything else under your nails is also a huge turn off. They don't know where your hands have been and seeing that under your nails will often cause her to expect the worst and won't want to touch you. So, <u>clean</u> <u>your</u> <u>nails</u>.

Get a scrub brush for cleaning your hands and nails, if your occupation or hobbies cause your hands to become that dirty. Get a good hand cleaner as well.

My nails are cut short, just above the "quick" or the nail bed. Because of my massage work, keeping them this short keeps me from accidently scratching someone and makes it more comfortable for my clients. Not everyone will want their nails this short. Your choice.

After I clip all of my nails down on both hands, I then use a coarse nail file to smooth the rough edges lightly. This takes down the sharp edge left from the clippers. Next, a finer grit to smooth out the edges, and the area the coarse nail file went over.

This is where most men can stop, though I take it a step further to smooth and round the edges to where they won't scratch someone, unintentionally, with a fine grit nail file, and then buff the edge. This keeps the edge smooth and I rarely have cracks or breaks in the nails. Take care of your finger nails. The ladies <u>WILL</u> notice.

Handshakes

Have you ever tried to shake hands with *The Incredible Hulk*? I haven't either, though I have had guys that thought they were *The Hulk* or maybe his cousin for how hard they squeezed.

This is a big *no-no* in social interactions. Squeezing someone's hand so hard it hurts, is usually a sign that the person is insecure and/or is attempting to establish dominance through brute force.

Realize that if you are this guy and you crush a man or woman's hand in yours as you meet them for the first time, you will not leave a good impression.

Instead of bullying by crushing handshake, take a different approach. Learn to give a good, genuine handshake that will be memorable and positive to the person for how firm, yet polite it was.

The handshake has been used as a greeting as far back as the 5th century BC. Yes, the handshake has been used for a long time.

Knowing how to do it well for your country is a very good idea. Here in the west, our handshakes are often stronger and more firm.

In Asia and the middle-east, the handshakes are more weak and usually between men. Also in the west, handshakes are more often used by men than women in casual, non-business, situations.

In the East, the handshake is usually only used among men.

So how do you give an appropriate handshake then? The handshake isn't a complicated gesture. If you aren't familiar with the handshake, look up *"how to give a handshake"* on *YouTube* and you will find a few videos to choose from.

When you are familiar with the basics of a handshake we can move on to the finer points of giving and receiving a good handshake.

A good handshake can show the person you are shaking hands with respect and make a good first impression.

When you approach the person, male or female, greet them (*"Hello, I'm Matthew..."*) if you don't know them and by name, introduce yourself, if you know their name greet them with their name (*"John, good to see you again..."*). Extend your hand for the handshake, looking the other person in the eye. They will usually take your hand and grasp it, execute a single downward pump, and release. Sounds simple, right?

There are some particulars that I want to bring up to make sure that the handshake is memorable. Make sure that the web of your hand and the web of their hand are firmly touching. Grasp their hand and once the webs of your hands are firmly touching, finish your grip. Not before.

By you pushing your hand into theirs until the webs of your hands touch, you will get a good mutual connection for the handshake, you show your confidence to the other person.

You be the one to make the gesture of pushing your hand into theirs. They may not know or trust you at this point. By you taking the lead it helps to get their attention.

Next, remember to grasp with gentle and firm pressure when shaking hands with a woman, matching the pressure if she increases it. Give a firm handshake to a man and match the pressure of his grip if it is added. This shows respect to the other person.

From personal experience and in speaking with many people over the past few decades, a weak *"dead fish"* (limp, clammy and effeminate) handshake doesn't inspire confidence in the other person any more than the *"bone crusher"* handshake.

One final skill I want to add to the handshake is *"insurance."* When a person you don't know wants to shake your hand, there can sometimes be a test of wills as the connection of the handshake is made and muscles flex, each person doing what they can to *"prove their masculinity"* to the other party.

This is crap. It really is. If you or anyone has to *"prove their masculinity"* by crushing another person's hand, they are insecure and a bully. Now, how do you protect yourself against this? It is super simple.

All you do is as the handshake is made; extend (point) your index (pointer) finger slightly towards the wrist of the other person as you complete the handshake.

Looking from the side it will look like your finger is pointing to the bottom of their wrist. This changes the alignment of the bones in your hand. If an attempt is made to *"crush"* your hand, the crusher will find it much harder to crush your hand than before.

By flexing your hand against the *"crush"* you will have a better chance of getting away without injury.

Respect the Bubble

Have you ever had someone you didn't know come right up to you and stand directly in front of you to where your shoes were *toe-to-toe*?

The majority of people that I've worked with, when asked this question, have never had this happen to them before.

It is super creepy and uncomfortable to most people. To add to the discomfort, look the other person in the eye the whole time that you are standing *toe-to-toe*.

In my trainings, this is one of the experiences I make sure that <u>each</u> of the participants has.

There needs to be the <u>emotional</u> and <u>physical</u> understanding, <u>not</u> just an <u>intellectual</u> one, of what goes on in a woman when *you*, the man, walk up to her and stand right in front of her staring her in the eyes. It is <u>SUPER</u> <u>CREEPY</u>!!!

It is almost overpowering to people when you get into their space, usually within elbow reach, in front of them. This is where they only allow close friends, family and lovers inside that area.

When you experience that reaction within your gut and your brain when you are <u>that</u> <u>close</u> to someone else, especially another man (provided that you aren't attracted to that man), you will begin to understand that staying outside of a person's *bubble* is very important when beginning to create *rapport* or a connection with them.

I'm not saying that you need to stay at two arms lengths at all times. What I am saying is that you need to watch for the signs of when it is *"ok"* to approach and when it isn't. A simple way to know when to approach is to make eye contact.

When eye contact is made and a smile is seen, even if it isn't a big smile, you can enter closer and then say *"Hi."* Please, Please, Please don't sneak up on her. <u>UGH</u>!

When I was younger (think *teenager*) I thought it was funny to sneak up on girls and surprise them with my being so close.

Though it was funny to me at the time, I now realize that I screwed up on a large number of awesome opportunities because I was, for the most part, *social/dating* clueless.

So please, don't approach her from an angle where she can't see you coming and surprise her. She won't be pleased and will feel it's quite *creepy*. Also, make a point to approach her from other angles where she can see you, rather than directly in front of her.

You are not (*hopefully*) a predator stalking your prey. You want to approach casually, with confidence, and simply begin a conversation. Remember these things and the approach becomes that much easier to accomplish. Remember; *"Respect the Bubble."*

CHAPTER 6 – UNCOMMON COMMON SENSE

You have heard of *"Common Sense"* before, right? When I was growing up I often heard my mom getting after me or my grandma telling me:

"Well you should know this. It's common sense after all."

<u>*Guess what:*</u> Common Sense isn't that common any more. Take each area with a grain of salt (or grain of <u>assault</u> if that suits you) and recognize that not everyone grew up as you did. We all come from different backgrounds, so it is important to have a common reference point helps us to build from. Let's begin.

Cleanliness

Yes, I am bringing this up. No, it is not *common sense*. *Common sense* needs to be relabeled to *"uncommon common sense"* to describe it better. *Common sense* seems to be gone from our society and the world in general these days. So, yes, I am bringing this up.

When I was going through basic training in the *United States Army* a few decades ago, we had classes in the first couple of weeks where we would learn the basics of hygiene and how to clean ourselves.

Yes, this was a class that all soldiers had as they were going through *basic training*. The reason for this was that each soldier had a different cultural background and home learning environment.

When you have that many people living together, some soldiers have different levels of *"acceptable"* cleanliness and hygiene and the barracks could get quite ripe very quickly.

These classes showed everyone what the appropriate level of cleanliness was and how to implement this in their daily personal cleaning practices.

If you didn't clean yourself, they might just hose you down and scrub you. I'm Serious!!!

First off: when you *"clean"* yourself, please, take a shower or a bath, when possible, to get your entire body wet and well soaped and rinsed. If you are heavier, spend the time to get all the cracks and crevices not only wet, yet well soaped and rinsed.

As a massage therapist I have worked on big people and when they are active or inactive and sweating for a few days without a shower, they tend to stink. Bad! (So does everyone that doesn't shower for days, yet it's worse when the person is heavier and can't reach all those areas as easily!)

When they shower or bathe and don't get all the cracks and crevices clean, it is HELL for a massage therapist having to deal with the smell while doing body work.

So please, please, please clean yourself well; everyone around you will appreciate it, even when <u>you</u> can't tell the difference.

When I shower, I personally use antibacterial soaps (*Dial* is my *go-to*) for most of my showers. I also will occasionally use body washes (*Irish Spring* is one of my favorites) or special hand crafted soaps that have a masculine fragrance.

I will wash with the *Dial* first and then a second washing with the other soap across my torso, neck and face. This gives a nice extra scent that gets me great results when a lady wants to give me a hug. She smells that light scent on my neck or chest. The results are appreciated.

<u>*Next:*</u> Wash Your Hair!!! If you have hair, – wash it. If you have hair anywhere on your body, it is a good idea to wash those areas. If you have had hair removed in the past, wash the areas where hair used to be. <u>Simple</u>. <u>Straight forward</u>.

<u>Please</u>, <u>please</u>, <u>please</u> wash your hair. I have seen too many guys simply put water on their hair to style it and expect that to be good enough.

The oil and grease still shows through. Some of us are oilier than others. That's life. We deal with it.

Because of these differences, there are shampoos that also work to address these differences. Grab a shampoo that works for you. I personally like to use Head and Shoulders with a shampoo and conditioner combo.

My hair is short and I don't have the issues with static or my hair sticking out, it does already and is the reason I keep it short.

I will then style my hair after the shower with a product (*pomade* or *gel*) to get the look that I am wanting. Some days my hair doesn't seem to be styled the way that I want. These are hat days.

Some days are hat days anyway. Accept it. You don't have to get all dressed up every day. However, when you do, take the time to look good and you will impress the ladies.

When you are done with your showers or baths, please, take the time to use deodorant. We, as humans, tend to get a bit smelly under the armpits as time passes.

Taking a shower isn't enough. You should use a deodorant as well to *"stink purty."* Just don't overdo the aftershave and cologne! You and your date and the world around you will thank you.

While you're at it, pay attention to the appearance of your living space, including your car. Clear the clutter. Neatness in your surroundings is a reflection of your inner life and mental state.

Don't worry about keeping perfect order, though, for you or your date. It's okay to cut yourself (and her) some slack if things aren't perfect. Close enough counts here.

By taking the time to make sure that you are properly cleaned, you will demonstrate to the world around you the pride you have in your appearance.

That, my friends, is a sign of self-confidence. Keep up the good work and keep clean. The people around you <u>DO</u> appreciate it.

Speak and Be Heard

Have you ever tried to shout to a friend across a room full of people that are dancing to loud music?

Did your friend hear you? I am thinking that it didn't work too well when you were shouting. Kind of like spitting in the wind. It doesn't do a whole lot that is productive.

The same can be said for mumbling to a woman you just met. When she can't hear you from three feet away with no background noise, we know that is not going to turn out well. Learning how to speak and when to speak is an important skill.

So where do you start? How do you learn the skill of learning when to speak? How do you learn how to speak? Knowing when to speak is something that comes with practice, lots of conversations, and a sense of timing.

What I mean by this is that, when you listen to another person speaking, there are natural pauses where you can add comments without interrupting them.

These pauses usually show up as the person is either getting ready to take a breath or after they have made a statement and they are gathering their thoughts for the next statement or tirade. This depends on what they are talking about. This is a simple explanation of when to make the statement.

The *"how to speak"* portion is *common sense*. And we know that isn't so common any more. When you are facing a person such as your employer, do you mumble? Do you look at your shoes and speak at the floor? If you don't, congratulations, you have a good start for *"how to speak"* with a woman you are interested in.

Want to be heard when you speak to someone? First off, open your mouth. Speaking through mostly closed lips is a no-no. That doesn't work too well in being heard.

Next is looking at the person you are speaking to. When you look away, up or down, your words are not carried to their ears the same way as if you are looking at them when speaking. The person can't hear you as well.

When you are speaking to a woman, please don't speak to her chest. I know that sounds funny, yet when an attractive woman chooses to expose her cleavage to the viewing of the world at large, it can be distracting. It is also deliberate. They are an advertisement.

Because, after all, they're *boobs*. And everyone likes *boobs*, right? So...*boobs*...don't talk to them during the conversation, focus on her eyes. Her *boobs* don't have eyes so don't try to keep eye contact with them.

Look her in the eyes. That is a better thing to focus on...at least during the present conversation.

Close Your Mouth and Listen
Ever tried to listen to someone else talking while you were talking? It doesn't work too well. When you are talking while someone else is talking your voice prevents you from listening. No, really, it's true. Sounds like *common sense*, right? Well...yeah, all that about *uncommon-common sense*. The key to being a good conversationalist is to keep your mouth shut until it is needed to open.

In **Chapter 8** I will be covering the skills needed to ask the questions that allow you to be a stimulating conversationalist. Until then, we will be working on learning to keep our mouths shut so we can hear.

Keeping your mouth shut while the other person speaks and keeping eye contact will help you make more of a connection with the other person. (*Remember*: *This is for the culture of the West. Asian/East cultures are a bit different.*

Remember to research the culture of other people before you go and date the women there. Not only will it save you some pit-falls, it will also build respect for you having taken the time to look up and research that material to prevent misunderstandings.)

These skills can be used in your interaction with everyone you meet. Try them out on friends, family, co-workers, people at the gym and anyone you meet throughout the day.

These skills of keeping your mouth shut, most of the time, will allow you to listen to the other person to talk about their favorite person…*themselves*. This is how you can learn about the other person and what is going on in their world and what they want you to know.

Asking questions will help you to get the answers you are wanting. The other person usually won't volunteer information unless you are asking and listening to the answers they give you.

Additionally: when the other person has stopped talking after they have asked you a question or made a statement, PAUSE for just a second or so before answering.

Often times when another person is speaking with us, something catches our attention, and we formulate a response while they are speaking.

Instead of truly listening to the other person, we are waiting to spring our response on them in the next break that they give us. This is often because we don't want to forget what we want to add to the conversation. Honestly, this is rude and juvenile.

When we aren't focused on the other person and instead focus on ourselves and what we want to say, we are being immature. Exercise a bit of self-control and wait until they are done speaking. As they finish, pause before answering.

The reason for the pause is that it gives the impression that you are thinking about and considering their words, even if you know what you are going to say.

The pause doesn't need to be very long, even a full second is enough. By speaking immediately it doesn't make the best impression. Once you know them, you can change this up a bit, yet _remember:_ to be a _good communicator_ you must be a _great_ _listener_.

Be On Time

This is a personal pet peeve of mine. Being on time is something that never really happened to me when growing up.

We were always late and never on time for ANYTHING! EVER! Doctor appointments, church meetings, getting to school in the mornings, parties and family gatherings. All of these. We were late.

The habit continued with me when I got married and began to grow my family. After nearly fifteen years of this, I bought my first business and all of a sudden I became fanatical about being on time. It was cool.

Since I've been divorced, I've worked to keep this habit going. When my kids are lagging behind in getting ready in the morning or when we have an appointment, I am quite the *Drill Sergeant* to keep us on schedule. It doesn't always work because kids are kids, yet for myself, I am still a stickler for being on time.

To me, being on time shows respect for the person you are meeting as well as for yourself. It might be for business or even hanging out with friends for lunch.

To me, it doesn't matter. I am the one that is in charge of myself. I am the only one who I can control.

Because of this, I feel that when I am on time I am fulfilling my part of the contract of us agreeing to meet at a certain time. This is respect for the other person, which is important. It is also having respect for myself, which can be more important.

Sometimes, life happens. In these cases, I always make sure to call the other person, rather than having them wait, not knowing if I will show up or if plans have changed.

I have to be the example. There is a great quote from Mahatma Gandhi:

"We must become the change we want to see in the world."

It is the philosophy I live by.

How can I expect someone else to be on time if I'm not going to be on time? When I am on time I am respecting the other person I am meeting and being the example of how I want them and others around us to act.

We are the example, even when we don't see the other people affected by our actions.

How and When to Touch

I think I could write another entire book just on touch and touching.

Touching is essential for healthy growth and development throughout our lives, especially during infancy and through childhood we need healthy touch to grow up emotionally healthy.

It is only natural to want to continue to touch another person as we get older. The problem with that is that most people, the way they were raised and due to our culture, don't want to touch or be touched back unless they know you. Even then, there are many restrictions.

There are some types of touch that are acceptable, and others that aren't. I'm not just talking about a grope or pinch as a lady passes by (which is, in my opinion, the sign that a person is rude, immature and boorish.)

A man can caress a woman with his eyes. Using your skills of good eye contact and appropriate choices of words, you then can earn the right to touch and not be rejected. The ones who pinch and grope do so because they won't be able to have the chance to touch her any other way.

Touching a woman you have just met is something that needs <u>LOTS</u> of practice to become comfortable with, if you don't already do this.

The *touching* I am speaking of is <u>only</u> touching her forearm and upper arm, between the elbow and below the shoulder.

The touching that you are doing needs to be done subtly and casually with the palm up or palm showing, moving naturally, as if you do this whenever you talk to people.

"It is natural for you to touch." This needs to be your mindset from now on. Touching allows people to connect on a physical level that will add to the mental and emotional components of *rapport.*

Rapport is an emotional connection where trust is built and closeness is created. By creating this *rapport* you are helping her to feel comfortable around you.

Touching outside of these areas when you first meet someone, and are not familiar with how to touch, is a *no-no.*

<u>Remember to reach out with your palm up, fingers extended.</u> This will help show sincerity and openness. Touching her hands, unless it is a handshake, right off the bat will send up warning flags.

Women are *"touchers."* Women, for the most part, are much more used to touching other people than men are in the *United States* cultural norm.

Because of this, it is important for men to understand that touching is familiar to women as a way of connecting with other people. They not only do this to other women; they also do this to men when they feel comfortable.

I love to watch people.

When you watch people, you will see certain patterns of behavior. One pattern that has always stood out to me is that women will touch each other's hands and arms often, when with a group of close friends.

They will do this to get attention or to emphasize a point. Watch for when women do this. They never look at their hand when touching the other woman. They also touch with their fingertips and occasionally will gently squeeze the other woman's arm. <u>They</u> <u>Do</u> <u>Not</u> <u>Grab</u> them roughly or with a strong grip.

<u>Pay attention</u>. Watch how women touch each other. It is an excellent lesson for guys to follow. Don't look at your hand as you go to touch a woman.

Looking at your hand makes the movement look as if you are uncertain and unaccustomed to touching a woman. Focus on watching her face and her eyes when you touch her arm.

Use your peripheral vision to see where you want to touch and to stay on target. I will often reach out to her, touching her arm, as I start the conversation: *"Hi, it's so good to see you here. Didn't I see you last week at Adam's party?"* as I ask this question, I will reach out and have my palm up and touch her forearm on the underside. (Don't make up a scenario and lie to get an opening.)

Be genuine. If you weren't at a party and didn't see her, simply ask another question.) When I touch her she will often reach back and touch my arm when I am genuine and have <u>NO</u> agenda, other than getting to know about her.

Watch women who are friends when they talk, they do very similar things. By using touch easily and naturally you can quickly build the trust that is needed to build a relationship.

BRUSH YOUR TEETH!!!

Is this really that hard? Have you looked at people's teeth? I mean really looked at them when they smile? Pay attention to this part of their facial anatomy the next time someone smiles at you.

What shape are their teeth? What condition are their gums in? Are they red and swollen or a healthy pink? What about food, is any stuck in their teeth? Are the teeth decayed or damaged? Are their teeth even <u>BRUSHED</u> within the past week?

Having good dental hygiene practices is a good way to keep your smile beautiful and attractive. Flossing at least daily is also key to good tooth and gum health that can make you look years younger and keep root canals at bay. I use flossing picks, the good quality ones. They make this task easier than using dental floss in most cases.

Not taking care of your teeth will often cause you to be self-conscious of your smile and not give the full smile to people. This often causes people to be less open and friendly when you don't smile completely. It can also be suspicious.

Watching for teeth issues also can give you an idea of possible health issues a person might have.

I was at a seminar a few months back and saw a pretty, thin blond that was standing in the back of the room.

She had her feet in a ballet position that I recognized from when I took ballet many years ago. (Taking a ballet class as a straight guy is a <u>great</u> way to meet ladies. Most of the men that are in ballet classes these days are gay, and the ladies are usually very friendly when you are <u>sincere</u> about learning ballet *and* show some aptitude and skill…it doesn't hurt that you are straight too.)

I noticed when she smiled big, that she was missing most of her molars. Later that week, I brought this up to a doctor friend of mine, and she told me the woman could be *bulimic* (an eating disorder that usually has the person eating a large amount of food and then purging or vomiting it back up) and that the practice of purgint, over time, will destroy the teeth from the stomach acid constantly attacking the protective enamel of the teeth.

This was a good lesson for me in learning about watching for signs about a person's body. It is good to learn about the signs; it is also good to learn what these signs mean and not to assume or guess if you aren't familiar with the signs.

Since we are on the subject of brushing your teeth, I want to address the issue of bad breath. I mentioned brushing teeth in **Chapter 5** and briefly mentioned bad breath. Bad breath can come from a variety of health disorders.

Digestive problems can frequently cause one's breath to be bad soon after brushing one's teeth. Though you can't always be rid of the bad breath, what you can do is take steps to eliminate as many causes as possible.

Brushing your tongue can be done to help with bad breath and can be added when you brush your teeth.

There are *"tongue scrapers"* available from most drugstores or supermarkets with a pharmacy area. These can help you to clean your mouth of more buildup that can cause bad breath. I personally don't use a tongue scraper. I simply brush my tongue as the final step after brushing my teeth.

All you need to do is scrub and brush the tongue area with your toothbrush to scrub away anything sitting on the surface, not going too far back because that sets off the gag reflex, and then rinsing your mouth and tooth brush afterwards to be ready for next time. That's it.

Make sure that before you go out, you brush your teeth and tongue to keep your breath fresh. It never hurts to have gum or mints as well…just in case.

CHAPTER 7 – LISTENING SKILLS

Everybody is unique. This is something we all know, even when we don't think about it. We all have differences and all have experiences in our lives different from others around us. That is life. Since we are all (last time I checked) humans, we can only experience things from so many perspectives. There is an old saying:

"There is nothing new under the sun."

This is especially true for us humans. By sharing our experiences, we find out that even though we seem quite different, we all share the human experience of life. That can bring us together…when we know how to relate to other people.

Thinker or Feeler

People's minds tend to fit into two simple categories: *Thinker* and *Feeler*. Yes, I know that this is an over simplification, and yet, why make communication more difficult than it has to be? Communication is all around us and we often overlook the simple things that can help us to communicate better.

The best way I have found to discover if the person is a *Thinker* or a *Feeler* is to listen to them. I know. Wild, right?

Yes, listening is incredibly important in being able to understand the words the other person is saying to you. I want to be clear here: *The words that are important are the ones that show you what style of communication the person uses.*

For example: If you ask someone how work was today and they give you a specific run down of all of the little details of work and what each task was...they're a *Thinker.*

If they instead tell you about how hard or fun or rewarding the day was and how it made them feel, either with feelings or body sensations, then chances are that they are a *Feeler.*

Thinkers best interact with the world in a logical and rational way. They think things through, using their reasoning abilities to figure out problems, and they are very *"brain"* oriented.

They pretty much don't stop thinking...ever. Engineers and pilots, doctors and mathematicians.

This also describes many men. I know, surprising, right? Yes, most men are *Thinkers*, and they are best communicated with verbally in a more logical and rational way. Most men stay away from expressing any feelings that make them feel vulnerable. They don't like or understand feeling vulnerable and don't want to be judged for feeling these strange things called *"emotions".*

Most communication for them doesn't have to do with feelings. They are more likely to avoid talking about feelings and want to have a logical reason why they do something, even when that reason is because they are feeling an emotion.

Feelers interact with the world in a way that is often more carefree than the *Thinkers*. *Feelers* are the artists, the musicians (some of them), care givers, creative people who want to work with their hands, the people who rely on their bodies to express their message, and their work reflects this.

Athletes and dancers tend to be *Feelers*. *Feelers* are very in tune with their bodies and the emotions that course through them. Artists are often times in tune with their feelings, as well as musicians, and want to creat a *feeling* from the works they produce.

In a conflict, *Feelers* are more likely to respond with emotional statements rather than logical ones. *Feelers* are confusing to the *Thinkers*, the same way that *Thinkers* are confusing to *Feelers*.

The reason I am bringing this up is that *Thinkers* and *Feelers* often use different words to explain the same thing.

Even though they use the same language, *Thinkers* and *Feelers* will express themselves in different ways to explain the same experience.

The *Thinker* will be straight and to the point, while the *Feeler* will usually tell a story that helps you understand how they are feeling and what they experienced.

When speaking with someone that is a *Thinker* or a *Feeler* you can quickly know how best to relate to them. As you recognize their *"style"* of communication you can change your *"style"* of communicating to fit theirs.

I was trained as a linguist in the military. I was also trained as an interpreter and an interrogator. Because of this, I have seen patterns that have been showing up when people switch between these *"styles"* of communication.

I like to look at these as different *"languages"* rather than *"styles"*. Because of this I will deliberately change my *"language"* to fit with the person I am speaking to.

Are they speaking the *"Feeler"* or the *"Thinker"* language? I simply switch my words and *"language"* to theirs and it is amazing how much clearer the message gets through to them.

As a linguist, I learned to speak other languages in order to better communicate with the people that speak those languages. What you are doing as you learn the *"language"* of the other person, is understanding how they think and process information. As you change your *"language"* to match theirs, you will now be more like them. This builds *rapport* and shows the other person that *"you really do understand."*

Try it and you will quickly realize that it changes the quality of your communication.

Learning Languages

There are five main communication modes, what I call *"Learning Languages"*: **Talker/Listener**, **Visual**, **Feeling/Touch**, **Taste** and **Smell**. We'll cover the first three: **Talker/Listener**, **Visual** and **Feeling/Touch**. The **Taste** and **Smell** *"languages"* are important; yet won't be covered at this time.

It doesn't matter what *"learning language"* you use to communicate. When people use the words associated with your *"language,"* it will be easier for them to understand you. It will also help you to get through to them when they are upset or feeling extra emotional.

Logic doesn't work well when interacting with emotions. Being able to use their *"language"* style gets through to them so much better, it seems like magic. Try it and see.

Talker and Listener
Let's start with the *Talker/Listener* language.

Talker/Listener language users tend to talk themselves through problems; they prefer to be verbally told what to do and are better learners when lectures are used in school.

These people that are more *Talker/Listeners* will want to talk their problems out and are usually excellent listeners. When under stress the *Talker/Listeners* will often use words and phrases that are associated with their learning *"language"*:

"Sounds like", *"I hear you"*, *"I'm getting nothing but static"*, *"that rings a bell"*, *"listen to me"*, *"talk to me"*, *"I can't hear what you are saying"*, *"speak up"*, *"help me understand what you are saying"*.

The *Talker/Listener's* life revolves around listening and talking. They will often have music playing in the background and are more likely interested in the spoken word than the written word.

By understanding the learning *"language"* of the person, you can then use this information to choose how to best interact with them.

Interact with the *Talker/Listener* by going to a concert, a musical, open-mike night at a local coffee shop or simply spending time for conversation with your ears open and an attitude of being ready to hear them.

This will mean the world to them when they need to share something that has been on their mind. The *Talker/Listener* explores the world through these senses.

When you can connect with a person in the way that they perceive the world, you can build trust and feelings of connection with them at the deepest emotional levels.

Visual

Visual learners want to see what it is they are supposed to do. They work better when they can get a *picture* of the outcome desired and tend to use words that describe that *picture* in their own mind. They use words to convey that *picture* to another person so they are able to *"see"* the same picture.

The words and phrases that are often associated with a *Visual* learner are:

"I can see your perspective", "look at it as if you were me", "I'm just feeling blue", "I clearly don't understand", "look at this", "I don't see it like you do", "Isn't it clear to you", "Don't you see what I am saying?", "If you just looked at it from my point of view".

These are all very *Visual* oriented words and statements. They describe the way that the other person is thinking.

Connecting is being able to understand how people think, and to show that person that you are like them. You are the same. Using these *"learning languages"* can help you to create deeper connections with people and build stronger relationships.

Being a *Visual* learner myself, I have found that I relate very easily to people that are also *Visual* learners. We tend to use words that relate well with others of our *"language."*

Remember: *Subtlety is the key. Don't change all of your words to match her style. Match the words she uses and fit the rest through the conversation. It is common for the types of words to change as a conversation covers different topics. Simply adapt and change as she does.*

Feeling and Touch

This area is broken up into two areas for good reason. The *Touch* part is for those who are more in tune with their bodies.

Those who are athletic, or are athletes of any kind, (dancers, extreme sports, martial arts, professional and amateur) tend to have a strong connection with their body. They live through the intimate connection to their bodies to the point that their thinking patterns reflect this *body connection*.

They will use words and phrases like:

"This is hard," "I can't hold on","I can't make the connection","Let's work together","Walk in my shoes and you will understand."

These people will often have very good body awareness and will often use their hands to explain sizes and shapes and move around as they talk and tell stories.

The next area is *Feeling* and no, it doesn't mean that they cry a lot...not necessarily anyway.

Those that have more of an emotional connection with their mind often have a connection to their body as well.

Since these go so well together, their words also tend to work together when they are expressing themselves.

Some of their words and phrases are:

"I've got a bad feeling about this", *"How do you feel about this?"*, *"If you were in my place, how would that make you feel?"*, *"I can understand how you feel"*, *"How do you feel about working together?"*

These phrases all have the *"feel"* part to them for good reason.

Those who are *Feelers* go by their feelings for the majority of their decisions. Earlier we discussed *"Thinkers and Feelers"*; and these types of people would definitely be the *Feelers*.

The interesting thing is that even though there are many different ways to *understand* people and relate to them, understand that these *Languages* and categories are only guidelines to help you understand that everyone is unique.

You can't expect to understand and know how every person communicates within a few minutes of meeting them.

Even though *I* can often get a good feeling for a person soon after meeting them, I then <u>need</u> to spend a lot of time with them to better understand them and fine tune the communication I have with them.

In order to get a deeper connection that ties in perfectly with listening skills, we are going to learn *"Reflective Listening."*

Reflective Listening

Have you ever looked in a mirror? Come on, you can admit it, you have. I have lots of times, and so have all of us reading this (except the vampires. They can't see themselves in mirrors...except for the sparkly ones!)

Have you ever thought about how mirrors work? The glass is transparent to the light, and as the light goes through the glass it hits the silvered back to bounce back out. What you are seeing in the reflection is a virtual image of you. Now why am I talking about a mirror?

Just the way that a mirror can bounce back the image to your eyes, when you are having a conversation with someone, it is good to *"bounce back"* some of what they have said to their ears. The reason for this is that it confirms that you were listening.

Yes, listening is a very important part of a conversation, and by using this simple technique of reflective listening, you can prove to a person that you were listening to what they just said.

It is also a great tool to interrupt someone with in a way that won't offend them. One way you could interrupt would be:

If two women were talking about the ski resort in *Brian Head, Utah* being closed for the next three weeks you could interrupt with:

"So, hold on a sec, you just said that the ski resort is closed for the next three weeks? Really? Do you know why?"

At this point you turn it back to them and wait for a response.

By interrupting and asking the question at the same time you were asking to get clear on what they just said, and yet also proving that you were listening to the words they said.

A great side benefit of interrupting in this way is that it doesn't usually offend the person that was talking. (unless you are easedropping and it's none of your business.)

When you are asking them for clarification and they know you are listening they are happy to give you the additional information.

Adding It All Together

Do you know how to dance? I mean with a partner, not flailing your arms and jumping around on the dance floor by yourself. If you do, then you know that there are usually two parts in a couples dance.

The male part or the *lead* and the female part or the *follow* are those two parts. In order to make sure that you dance well and smoothly, you should know both the *lead* and the *follow* parts and be able to work together with your partner to make the dance flow.

Being able to use your skills of *recognizing how a person thinks* and *what their learning language is* and then *listening intently to what they have to say*, all at the same time will take quite a bit of work.

Yes, it will take effort. These *skills*, and yes, they are *skills*, should be practiced one at a time until each is mastered. Once you have the first, move on to the next *skill*.

When you are able to weave these *skills* together, you will be able to talk to a woman in conversation and be able to get an idea of how she thinks and how compatible you both could be in a short amount of time.

The best way for two people to get to know each other is to talk. *Face-to-Face* is best, yet the phone is also quite helpful for this.

These *skills* help you to recognize how people interact with the world, and often how they are thinking as well.

Learning how other people think and process information has proved invaluable to me as a relationship skill. I know that with a little effort, you will be able to use these same skills to learn about and understand the ladies you meet (even if it's just a little better), and surprise them with how perceptive you can be.

CHAPTER 8 – CONVERSATIONS

Unless you have taken a journalism course or were military or government trained in questioning skills, (AKA: *Interrogation*) you most likely haven't learned how to ask questions in the most effective way to get information from a person.

This chapter will give you a better idea of what you need to be asking and how you need to phrase the questions to get the answers you are wanting.

The Who

No, it is not the band and not *The Doctor*! When I say *"Who,"* what is the first thing that pops into your mind?

An owl? Hopefully not. *"Who"* is the question that you want to know that will give you the answers about a person.

It sounds simple, and it is. We use it all the time, yet here I am making sure that you use all of these *"question words"* to get the answers that you are wanting in a conversation.

An example of this question would be:

"And who are you?" extending your hand to a woman at a party where people are introducing themselves.

"Who is that?" pointing over to a person. *"Is that Amy?"* You can then either go over and talk to the person or continue the conversation.

Chances are that you have been using the *"Who"* question for a <u>LONGGG</u> time. My question to you is: how well have you been using it with the other questions in a conversation?

The What

The *"What"* question is one that gets specific on a topic, person or object. It is very useful for getting information on where to go: *"What street was I supposed to turn on?"*

It is also useful for getting specific ideas on types of restaurants to go to on your date:

"What would you like to have for dinner tonight? I know a great Thai place as well as a Greek restaurant. What sounds good to you?"

"What" allows you to focus on the topic being discussed and allows you to get specific information needed to move to the next step. I will often use *"How"* with the *"What"* question. They are very complementary:

"What would you like to do for dinner tonight? Eat in or dine out? We can also go to a club that just opened downtown after dinner. How does that sound to you?"

Once you get used to being specific in your questions, they will flow very smoothly together. (*And yes, I do like ethnic foods!*)

The When

This question is usually used a couple of different ways during *"questioning"* to verify times, facts, and information about military troop movements and such.

The uses in civilian life are a lot more…casual.

"When" is a great question to ask when you want to verify when you're supposed to meet or pick a woman up for your date. Yes…very important!!!!!

An example of this question would be:

"When is the best time for me to pick you up tonight? 7 o'clock or 8?"

Asking a question this way gives options. It's okay to suggest a time range as a framework for what might work for both of you.

Everyone likes options; even when the man is supposed to be planning the date, the lady likes to be informed about options (especially if she has food allergies or other health challenges. <u>Guys, pay attention to these things</u>).

Another question:

"When are you off work?"

Gather information with the *"When"* question that you can apply to your plans for another time.

Gathering the right information and keeping track of it is a great way to earn brownie points.

"When is your birthday?" asked early in the relationship and remembered later will leave her even more impressed than normal at your attention to detail.

The Where

Crucial. Let me state this again: <u>CRUCIAL</u> in understanding where to meet a woman for your first date or to pick her up from her house when you earn that privilege.

"Where" might not be the most important question you can ask in your arsenal, however, you won't get anywhere until you learn to ask this question.

Make sure you are specific and that you are getting the correct answer. Double-check the info given so that you get it right the first time.

Showing up a half hour late because the address was wrong and your GPS didn't get it right is no excuse. Ask for directions if you need to. This is a thing that women will appreciate.

"Where" is a simple question that is often not asked, even out of courtesy, on where she would like to sit or to go? You, as the man, are supposed to make the preparations and direct where the date is going.

Taking charge doesn't mean you do not ask for her preference or input. Asking her preference is good manners. Letting her take the lead sometimes can be a refreshing change for both of you.

Being polite is very important when you are building a relationship and in keeping a relationship.

The Why

I don't use the *"Why"* very often, unless it is a question like *"Why don't we head over to this other party."*

The question *"Why"* is useful for what it is needed for; to answer a question about the reasoning behind an action. Using it to accuse, *"Why did you do that?"* or to criticize, *"Why can't you understand simple directions?"* is <u>poison</u> to a relationship. Instead think of ways to ask the *"Why"* question in more a more constructive manner.

"Why" can also be used to clarify an answer that was given. We all have questions when we are speaking to other people, whether we ask them or not.

Knowing how to ask the question in a way that will build the relationship is what we are wanting here. Such as:

"Hold on a sec, I have a question. Why did you say that you didn't want to go out tonight? I remembered that you had been feeling a little sick earlier. Is that why?"

Notice that I haven't accused or assumed. I am asking the question to get more clarity about the answer that was given. A <u>very</u> important thing to do.

The How

As I mentioned above, there are some of these questions that flow very smoothly together. I have found that the *"What"* and the *"How"* are quite complementary, working nicely together.

The *"How"* is asking for the way or the method something is going to be accomplished.

By asking *"How,"* we will be able to get the information needed to make the next choices to achieve our goal.

Whether it is date night or getting handyman stuff from the hardware store, it is all tied to the *"How"*. Being able to mix and match these questions will make your life much easier.

Putting It All Together

The challenges in communication often come from not enough information and assumptions coming from that lack.

By learning how to ask the questions needed to get that important information, the whole conversation and relationship process will flow easier.

Remember: *Women aren't men*. I know you are thinking *"DUH"*, yet hear me out. They don't think like men. <u>Don't expect them to think or act or answer questions like a man would.</u>

It is for <u>you</u> to be the interpreter of their words and to understand what it is they are wanting or saying. Asking the right questions will help ladies to be more patient with you, since you are making that effort, calmly. (Guys, keep calm and all will be ok. Refer to Breathe and Count, ***Chapter 3*** if necessary)

Learning to ask questions casually and skillfully will make that comprehension of what women are saying and wanting much easier for both parties.

Men: when I spoke earlier about the _"Learning Languages"_ and _"Thinker"_ or _"Feeler"_ style of people in **Chapter 7**, I was referring to how people think and process information.

Additionally there also seems to be two different _"Languages of the Sexes"_ which I have broken down into two languages: _"Man speak"_ and _"Woman speak."_

Yes, it is simple, that makes it easier for me and every other person out there to understand that doesn't have a PhD behind our names.

Women don't usually understand _"Man speak,"_ and guys don't usually understand _"Woman speak"_. The way we are getting past this is to ask questions.

Who, _What_, _When_, _Where_, _Why_ and _How_ questions are the tools we need to use to get the messages passed back and forth from _"Man speak"_ and translate into _"Woman speak"_ and back the other direction.

Use these questioning skills with everyone you talk to. That is the easiest way to become comfortable with the translations as well as getting to know someone. Enjoy.

CHAPTER 9 – REJECTION

Guys, I'm not going to beat around the bush with this one. Rejection is something that <u>YOU</u> choose to feel inside you. It is not something that a woman <u>does</u> to you.

It is something that is triggered from the way that a person treats you and that you internalize that rejection as a part of yourself.

It does not have to be that way. Rejection is something that doesn't have to hurt or cause you to want to run away in fear and hide under a rock.

I've been there. Too many times actually. When I realized that it was <u>me</u>, yes <u>me</u>, which was the problem, I then worked on improving who I was and my <u>own</u> views of my <u>own</u> self-worth, my confidence changed and rejection now is simply a bump in the road. It's no longer personal.

It's Not Personal

Have you ever personally known a police officer? These men and women have one of the toughest jobs in the world. Constantly dealing with the *dirtbags* of society on a daily basis. They don't see the world as you and I do.

They are always having to be on their guard and pay attention to the laws, the people around them, and how those both interract with each other.

One of the toughest things about this is that they stop seeing *people* as *people* after a while. They begin to see everyone as a potential *perp*, *perpetrator* or *dirtbag*.

Everyone becomes a *suspect* and they get so used to seeing this that they aren't always the most friendly of people…unless you are another officer. If you are another officer, well then, you're family.

As another officer, you would understand and have the same viewpoint. The reason that I am bringing this up, is that women have become jaded in a similar way.

Women have been hit on <u>thousands</u> and <u>thousands</u> of times over their lifetimes and they eventually start to group all men as *"suspects"*, guilty until proven innocent.

They learn a few ways to take care of these men, that they aren't interested in, with methods that aren't very pleasant to be on the receiving end of.

Usually, the more *needy, clingy, douchebaggy,* or *creepy* men appear, the stronger the response is. Understand this: **<u>It's not personal</u>**.

If they don't know you as a person, it's not personal. They are defending themselves the best way they know how from unwanted advances.

Defensive Mechanisms
Each woman has, from the time she hits puberty and sometimes before, become a sexual target to the males around her.

Once her eyes are opened to how boys and eventually men can be, she begins to categorize men in her own way.

Some of these categories include: *creeper, creepy old guy, player, douchebag, dick, asshole, hottie, sexy beast, nice guy, friend, BFF*... and the list goes on and on.

The more attractive she is, from what I have seen, the more she begins to see every man that approaches her as a potential *dirtbag*...oh, I mean a potential *creeper*.

Think about it. Attractive women are hit on thousands of times before they even hit twenty.

Because of this, they develop defensive mechanisms to the men that approach women in certain ways. Some of the defensive mechanisms are facial expressions, body language, cutting words and comments, using friends as a shield, etc.

The reason for this is because, to them, when you are rejected by a woman, it's not personal.

You have approached her in a similar manner to a *douchebag* from her past and she is simply responding to the message you were displaying to her.

Sound familiar?

How Women Protect Themselves: Words

The woman's tongue is her greatest weapon. Don't make this sexual because she will cut you deep and you will feel every cut she makes...with her words.

Just as I mentioned previously about a woman learning from a young age about dealing with men hitting on her, the skills they learned are ones that worked for her.

113

Sometimes she discovered that by calling a man a name or yelling at him or even making a gesture, she could deter some of the *creepers*.

Did it work all of the time? No. Some men didn't get the hint. (This is one thing that women seem to do over and over, hoping that the guy will get it. She *Hints*.)

Guys don't get hints. (No really, they don't get hints!) <u>Don't</u> <u>hint!</u> ***This is for ladies that are reading this.*** Instead, simply tell *guys* your thoughts and ask them to go away.

Because hints don't work with most men, the woman then can work with other skills, like volume.

Yes, shouting or screaming at a man in a public place tends to make his *balls* shrivel up and hide somewhere around his adam's apple as he becomes the center of attention to everyone around him, including other ladies.

This is simply another skill she has used in the past. If this happens to you, don't go running away or let your head hang low.

Simply smile or laugh and comment on the power of her lungs and walk away smiling and laughing. It changes the perspective of the people witnessing her outburst.

By your remaining in control, it will make her look out of control. *Remember:* Don't take it personally. (Also, when replying, don't make it personal, meaning don't make it a personal attack against her with words or actions. *Remember:* Don't take it personally.)

How Women Protect Themselves: Attitudes
Ever heard the term *"bitchy"*? If you haven't heard that term you either haven't been around women

before…meaning <u>EVER</u>, or you have grown up under a rock. Either way, I am introducing you to the term again.

The attitude of *"bitchy"* is one of a variety available to women as a defensive mechanism to protect them from the attention and advances of unwanted male suitors. (*That means*: guys that she thinks are *creepy* or *douchebags* or whatever.)

Attitudes come in a variety of flavors and colors. Please, recognize that these attitudes, when they are directed at a man, are usually because she is not wanting to be bothered, interrupted, or in other ways spoken to.

Once again: *Don't take it personally*. This is a defensive mechanism that is meant to keep unwanted males away from her. You don't know what is going on in her life and what might have happened earlier that day, week, month, or year.

Realize that you aren't there to irritate her. You are there to be social and to get to know the people who are open to your attention. If she doesn't want to be that person, then you move on and find someone who does want to be social with you.

No <u>DOES</u> Mean No

Ok, there has been some debate in the past on when *"No means No."* Let me put it simply. **No means No**. What part of the word *"No"* do you not understand?

There will be some men who will tell you that when she says *"No"* it means that you can keep pushing because she really doesn't mean it. Ugh! Idiots! These *"geniuses"* (Yes, that is <u>sarcasm</u>!) are either *date rapists* or *date rapists-waiting-to-happen*.

There are some perceptive guys who are recognizing that in some cases, let me emphasize the words <u>SOME GUYS</u> (these are usually experienced and knowledgable men who already know the signs to look for) who realize that the *"No"* was playful and not serious.

They know that when the other body language says *"No"*, they will respect that. If the rest of the body language and the voice tones and the facial expressions were saying more than the simple *"No"*, then they find out what she is really saying.

If you're reading mixed signals, keep it super simple: *"No"* means backing off, or checking in with the woman instead of assuming or pushing her.

She will appreciate your sensitivity, and the rebuilding momentum can be even better when all systems turn to a mutual *"Yes."*

I have been in situations where women I have dated have had some objections to how fast we were moving on a date. There were questions and some resistance.

I addressed the questions and continued forward, provided that the signals were positive, always paying close attention to her body language during the situation. I <u>ALWAYS</u> respect her body and her wishes.

When you respect her and go back to building the deeper relationship and help to move through any communication blocks, you will know when she is ready to say *"Yes."*

When you are paying attention to the situation with the woman and what she is saying and what she is doing, moving forward and becoming more sexual is a natural and positive thing.

I have noticed that, with me, when I have set the right mood, created the comfort and then escalated into sexual contact, I normally don't get resistance.

When I do get resistance, I know that I have missed something and need to go back and address it. I know that *"No means No."* It has never meant anything else to me. I hope that you will pay attention and remember that ***"No means No."***

When She Says Yes…

Alright, now we're talking! *"Yes"*, does mean yes…the question is now, what is she saying *"Yes"* to?

I'm not going to attempt to tell you how to go through the stages of *attraction* and *seduction* and teach you how to *escalate* the encounter with the woman to get her to the place where you can get imitate.

How you should respond to her when she says *"Yes"* at each stage is what I <u>am</u> going to focus on.

Have you ever seen a cute puppy that is so happy to see you? They are cute because of their size and their attitude. It's fun to play with a little creature that enjoys your company and wants to be around you.

It is, however, not as cute to have a full grown man acting like a puppy because a woman he met has said *"Yes"* to going out for coffee. Please! Guys! Act your age and man-up!

The mindset that I have learned to cultivate when I am dating is an expectation of *"Yes"*. Having that expectation is not arrogance. It is confidence. That confidence is what carries you to each succesive stage of the relationship.

The confidence that a man shows is very important to a woman. Women see confidence as very sexy. They see the lack of confidence as the opposite of sexy. Get it?

Be confident when around a woman and have the confidence that she will say *"Yes"* when you ask for her name, whether you can sit next to her, talk to her, get her number, or get a date.

Having the expectation of *"Yes"* as you progress to new stages of your relationship is at the same level as knowing that the sun will rise tomorrow.

Have confidence in yourself and know your value. And please, please, please… don't start doing the happy dance and jumping around when you get her phone number, email, or get the date… *at least until you are alone*. Good luck.

CHAPTER 10 – RECOGNIZING THE SIGNS

If we could see and recognize all of the signs that people are giving us through body language, we would have a completely different picture of the world.

With their voice tones, the words used, and all of the other tiny micro-expressions happening in real time on their faces, we get a more complete story of the events going on around us.

Earlier I spoke about how, *"All Behavior is Communication"*. You will realize that everyone has a story they are telling to the world. As you become more skilled, you will become more adept at deciphering the messages that everyone is giving off at a subconscious level.

The body constantly gives off the smallest hints and signals of our thoughts and feelings without our conscious control. Our job is to recognize what these signals mean.

Watch the series *"Lie to Me"* on <u>Netflix</u>. I love the first season the most. It clearly shows us, even though it is a bit dramatized, how subtle changes to a person's face can tell volumes of information. What are you saying unconsciously?

Actions speak louder than words. This is a <u>BIG</u> thing that *"Lie to Me"* taught me about behaviors.

Mouth Touch

Ok, this is cool. Have you ever been in a conversation with someone, especially with a woman, and she touches her mouth with a finger.

You keep on talking like nothing is wrong and as you keep going on and <u>on</u> and **on** about whatever it is that you are liking to talk about, most likely about yourself and how awesome you are, you notice that she then touches more of her fingers to her mouth, almost like she is keeping herself from saying something.

And then, because you are so awesome after all, you keep talking and <u>talking</u> and **talking** and her fist goes up to her mouth as you keep talking.

Then her hand drops, in defeat, and you notice a change that you can't explain in her. Has this happened to you?

Well, guess what. You just screwed up **BAD**. I mean <u>baaaaad</u>. When a woman touches her mouth, as I described, it is a sign that she wants to talk. She wants to say something that adds to the conversation.

As the signs progress she wants to say something even more and yet doesn't because it would seem rude.

Anyway, as the pressure builds, she will put a fist in front of her mouth to hold back the flood of what she wants to say.

When she is finally unable to deal with the pressure she will drop her hand in defeat. She now will not speak to you about that subject.

It is a great source of arguments and fights between couples. When you ask her: *"Hey honey, are you ok?"* and she says *"I'm fine."* You know the words of doom have been spoken.

How do you fix this? Well, first off, don't get into this position if you can avoid it. Second, you should be watching for the hints where she is touching her mouth or around her mouth and simply ask her *"Would you like to say something?"*

Sometimes she will decline, and yet if she is really interested in the conversation she will respond and marvel at your *psychic* powers of knowing when she wanted to say something.

Tell Me More

So there you are, talking to this beautiful lady and she pushes her hair behind her ear…what does it mean?

Well…in simple terms…it depends. Is she smiling? Is she looking at you with interest or with distain? So…this is where the body language takes a turn for the confusing.

Body language isn't as simple as it is shown in some books. It isn't simply looking at a person and mysteriously developing *Jedi Mind powers* of observation. It's more than that.

There is a thing called *"clustering"* where multiple body language *"tells"* or indicators let you know if those *"tells"* are saying the same thing. They let you know when the information that the person is showing through body language is accurate.

Going back to the beautiful lady pushing her hair behind her ear...when we see this we quickly check to see if her head is turned slightly to turn her ear towards you and exposing her neck to you. Next we check for her smile and her eye contact.

If all of these are present and her torso is facing you directly, you have a green light for continuing to talk.

Her touching of her ear is a sign that she likes what she is hearing and *"tell me more"*.

Yes, the body language can be this simple and straightforward. It can also be a bit more complicated, by the extra steps and *"tells"* that have to be interpreted.

Usually any time that someone is touching their ear as you are speaking to them is a sign that they want to hear more. However, what else they are saying through these gestures also needs to be recognized.

There are many signals that are given out all around us through body language.

All we have to do is to pay attention and recognize what it is that is being communicated.

Not Comfortable

Ever watched a little kid do the *"pee-pee"* dance? Legs crossed and little steps from one foot to the other; they're squirming if they're sitting in a chair, and usually having hands pressing on the groin area.

It is often the sign that a young child, that is potty trained, has to go pee.

This is also seen in women, to a more subtle degree, that are waiting in a long line at a concert or party where there is a long line of ladies waiting for the bathroom.

The reason that I am bringing this up is that these are signs of discomfort. Squirming or fidgeting, standing or sitting, playing with jewelry in a nervous way, rubbing their palms on their thighs, almost as if drying them off, are all signs of discomfort.

Have you seen these?

I'm sure you have. We've all seen these signs and yet we don't always recognize them on a conscious level.

Part of being a good communicator is recognizing the signs that are right in front of you and around you.

Learning to open your eyes and see what is there, is very important when watching body language.

There is a phenomenon called *"Change Blindness."* Check it out online if you want more in depth info.

The short version is this: *When things change in your environment around you, you don't always recognize what the changes are once they happen.*

For example, you have two pictures that have boats in them. They are both identical except one object, say a life jacket on the deck, which is in one picture and missing in the other picture.

When researchers showed people the two pictures either side by side or flashing from one picture to the other, they found that some people could see the differences quickly and others could never see the differences.

The reason that *Change Blindness* is important is that when we don't know what to look for we can often miss what is there in front of us the entire time.

Watching for some of the signs of discomfort you would see:

Not wanting to make eye contact, turning the torso away from the viewer, attempting to make oneself smaller through hunching, slouching, arms held close, and often holding hands together, repetitive touching, and many, many more.

There are so many things that can show the signs of discomfort. *The question is*: *Do you see the signs that are in front of your eyes?*

Real Smile vs. Fake Smile

You see her from across the room and you make eye contact. She smiles and then turns her head to look to the side.

You see the smile and assume that she is interested in talking to you. You decide to walk over and to talk to her. She continues to smile as you walk over, looking to the left and to the right as you get closer.

You introduce yourself as you get close to her and before you get her name she excuses herself and mysteriously has to go to the ladies room. What just happened?

Well…as we mentioned in the last section, what were you not seeing? Something that I did NOT know about women, before I decided to research it, was that they see nothing wrong with making an excuse (*AKA*: *lying*), when they don't want to make a public scene or to hurt someone's feelings.

With that understood, I also discovered that women will also have a public and social appearance that they will keep up even when they are uncomfortable. Just look at the torturous shoes they wear simply because they are *"cute."*

Smiles are part of the social appearance that they will keep up even when they are uncomfortable.

A woman will smile at another woman and they can pass the messages of how they are feeling with body language alone and both of them will understand the messages being shared.

Guys, on the other hand are generally clueless about what goes on with communication between women and often times between men and women. I know I used to be.

I still don't understand all of it, yet what I do know has made my life so much better when dating and interacting with women.

Smiles are a big part of the body language that helps women to get their message across to men and other woman from a distance.

The smile is a facial expression that is used around the world as a greeting and often displays the teeth when the full smile is showing.

Some things to be aware of though: there are a number of ways to smile that are correct in showing friendship, happiness and pleasure at seeing someone.

There are at least multiple wrong ways that give a different message than friendship, happiness and pleasure.

I'll only go into one *"smile"*. I will go over one that isn't showing the *"happy message"* even though it looks quite similar to the true smile.

The, what I call *"fake"* smile, is the smile that seems to be only with the mouth and the smile doesn't reach the eyes. The eyes are the giveaway that the smile is genuine.

Some people can fake the smile this way, by showing emotion in the eyes. This, however, doesn't seem genuine unless the person is feeling the emotions. (*Look at professional politicians.*)

There are many micro-expressions that make up the smile and when the smile is genuine, we see those micro-expressions.

The fake smiles are missing some of those micro-expressions when we look for them. They don't seem as genuine.

These micro-expressions are controlled by the subconscious and much harder to control at a conscious level. Lying is a conscious action.

If you are wondering if she is really interested in seeing you or meeting you, watch for the body language with the smile.

The head looking to the sides and torso turning away from you are all good signs that she is or isn't interested. You have to decide what to do now, based on that information.

She Touches You
Ok, now we're getting somewhere. You've been watching your body language. You have been asking the questions to get the information you are wanting from her.

You are inside of her *bubble* and her personal space. You touch her on the arm, palm up and arm extended.

Position your body so that it is not directly facing her as you speak to her, when you first meet her.

Stay slightly turned away from her until she turns her torso to face you directly, and then you also turn to face her. And then...when you make a witty comment...she touches your arm.

What do you do? Do you get a big grin on your face and look at where she touched you? Do you freeze? Panic? What is going through your mind when she touches you back? Hopefully the thought of:

"Good...she touched me back...I'm doing the right thing...keep on doing the right things and she will keep touching me."

<u>YES</u>! Realize that when she touches you, she is doing so to communicate that she is enjoying your company and that you are doing the right things to keep her interest.

When I realized these things and could consistently get my dates to touch me back, I was thrilled! I had it! I knew what I was doing! <u>YES</u>!!!

And then I realized that I still had work to do to take it further if I wanted to create more trust and to get intimate with her.

I wasn't there yet...however, I <u>had</u> arrived at a crucial point. I was at the point where I was getting results and when I kept my focus on what I was wanting, I was directing the flow of events to get the results that were important to me.

The pieces of the puzzle to how this whole *"dating and eventually sex thing"* were finally coming together. (no pun intended)

She Enters Your Space...

Alright, she touches you back as you banter back and forth. It is a good thing. You begin to get a feel for how comfortable she is by watching her body language and facial expressions and her eye contact. I know, it sounds like there is a lot to keep track of.

Initially it can seem overwhelming. As you practice and use these skills, more and more, they will become second nature for you to use. You will know what to do in the moment and it will simply seem *"right"* and you will progress to the next stages.

As for the personal space, what I have found and love to do to get inside of her personal space as well as to get her into my personal space is to go dancing.

"Dancing" you may say, *"I don't know how to dance or know anything about dancing!"*

Well, then learn. There are dance studios that teach *Salsa*, *Tango*, *Ballroom*, *Bachata*, and *Kizomba* in most communities.

If you don't have a dance school in your area, you might check with the community events center in your town to see if any classes are available or coming soon.

Dancing is not only *sexy* and *very attractive* to a woman; *it is the fastest way I've found to get her close to you, inside both of your bubbles, and to help build trust and comfort.*

I love dancing. I love when I can dance with my partner and they feel and read my movements as I lead them and they respond as if we are one person moving in harmony.

Dancing is a sexy and sensual experience that I find to be an ideal way to find out if my partner is compatable with me.

I enjoy dancing and when she moves with me as if we are sharing the same body...well...for me, that's about as much fun as you can possibly have with your clothes on.

I have taken classes in *Salsa* and some *Ballroom*, those are fun.

I much more like the *Kizomba* (key-samba) dancing because of the simplicity of it as well as the closeness that you are with your partner, chest to chest.

Learning to dance is *super sexy* when done right. Being that close to a woman, especially when you both are smelling good and feeling attraction, will build some positive responses through both of your body language and through conversation. Dancing is a great way to help change a simple experience into a relationship.

Enjoy.

CHAPTER 11 – FINAL ADVICE

All of the material we have covered so far is simply an overview of possibilities. Honest.

There is so much material that we can learn and so many areas for us to train and practice; we could spend many lifetimes attempting to learn everything there is.

Instead of spending lifetimes to learn and not do, take the time to learn enough to get started and experience your life <u>now</u> and learn as you go.

You will <u>never</u> learn **everything**. What you can do though, is to learn from mistakes and improve the person, who you are, every day.

Welcome to a bigger world with a brighter future filled with love and possibilities.

Pay Attention

Attention to detail. That is a military saying that has stuck with me over the years. When we are focusing on the little things we keep the big things from getting out of hand. It's usually the little things that get overlooked and they are the ones that cause the biggest problems when not addressed immediately.

When we make it a habit to pay attention to the details and the little things, it becomes a habit which will carry us through when we are under stress.

It is easy to pay attention to details when we are comfortable.

It is much harder to pay attention to all those little details when we are right in front of a beautiful woman and having to focus on her and what she is saying and what is going on around us. That, my friend, is stressful. President Lincoln said:

"When the time for action has come, the time for preparation has passed."

Practice your skills with everyone. Make it a habit to practice these skills when you aren't faced with the stress in the moment.

Utilize the scenario drills that we talked about in **Chapter 3** to prepare yourself for when you are talking to the ladies.

Here is some of the most important advice that I was ever given when I was learning how to talk to women:

"Talk to and treat an attractive woman like you would talk to and treat an unattractive woman. The skills don't change, the attitude doesn't change. She is a woman, talk to her."

That statement the most golden advice I was ever given. I have made the statement more *Politically Correct*. (The old statement was *"Talk to a pretty lady like you would an ugly one"*. Not the most politically correct, yet when I realized the value in this, it was a *game changer* for me.)

The reason that this was so powerful was when I realized that both of these women are both human and female.

They both want to be treated as valuable, even simply as a person. When I approached the idea of simply wanting to talk to her and learn something about her, it didn't matter which woman I spoke to.

I would use the exact same skills to learn about the attractive woman as well as the one that wasn't as attractive.

Yes, it's that simple. So pay attention and you will be successful. If I can do it, (*considering how clueless I was before I learned these skills*) anyone can do it.

Communication Is Constant

Everything you do and everything you say is being watched by the world around you. You can't get away from it.

Everyone else is doing the exact same thing, broadcasting and being watched, and they can't avoid it either. So what can you do about it?

You choose what message the world is receiving from you.

Since communication IS constant, why not change the message to one that is best for you? When I was younger and attempting (poorly) to convince ladies to like me, I was failing so hard. I was having NO luck at all. I was clueless and didn't know it.

Instead of finding out why I was having no luck, I got mad, blamed everyone else, and essentially felt sorry for myself and buried my sorrows in fantasy books and video games. Sound like anyone you know?

Fast forward a few decades. Everywhere I go, I am in charge. No, I don't own the world, yet I do control the world and the environment where I stand and as far as my arms reach.

That attitude and confidence in myself shows in how I hold my body and how I move. It is reflected in how I make eye contact and in how easy it is for me to have conversations with everyone and anyone.

I am in charge of my communication now. I work with *mentors* to further improve my communication skills and work to further increase the effect of my communication skills.

Yes, even *mentors* have *mentors*. The real *experts* seek out better *experts* to improve their abilities and skills.

Experts realize that the world around them won't stop for them and that they can't stop learning or they'll be left behind.

That desire for constant improvement also communicates to the world, and people around him, the message that the *expert* is important enough to invest in himself.

Experts put that message out to the world and the world responds. Messages are all around us.

The question is now, what is the message that you are putting out for the world to see?

You Are Awesome

Everyone has the potential to be awesome in something. I don't care if it is in cleaning toilets or in hitting home runs in the *World Series*. Each is useful in its own way.

You have something in you that is awesome that is waiting to be brought out. Do you know what that something is? You may not know now, yet I do know that there is something there.

By you first recognizing that you are awesome, you can then begin to develop and bring out that awesomeness.

A mentor of mine in the past had shared with me a *"holy book"* (it was kind of weird, about four inches thick and the color was a bright lime green...yeah, it was...different) from some obscure religion.

Even though the book was full of lots of stuff that I had absolutely no interest in, there were a few gems that he shared with me. He said, after showing me the reference in the book, that people are *"ripe and unripe fruits."*

Everyone has potential and not everyone is ready at the same time, just like a fruit tree's fruits. Though some may ripen faster, others may never ripen completely or in the right way.

This is life. We may never be ready or *"ripe"* for every occurrence or experience that we have in life, yet, that is what the learning process is for.

We become *"ripe"* through our life experiences and through learning. We are all *awesome*. We have to accept that we are *awesome*.

When we truly understand, accept <u>and</u> claim our *awesomeness*, the world will then also recognize our *awesomeness* and our lives will change as we become more *"ripe."* Enjoy the journey.

You <u>Can</u> Do This
Henry Ford said:

"Whether you think you can or think you can't, you're right."

You know…he had a point. He still does for that matter. Mr. Ford hit that nail right on the head. Our ability in life isn't dictated by our capability.

It is dictated by our willingness to do the uncomfortable things and to improve our lives through work and effort.

As we are willing, our capability and capacity increase. We all have skills. Some of us have skills that are a bit…different than the norm.

In **Chapter 1**, I talked about *"Demanding Your Best"* and in being the best person you can be and developing skills. Why did I mention it then? Why am I mentioning it now? When you have the mindset that *"I can do this,"* the world becomes your oyster.

You can pick and choose the pearls that are all around you and reap the rewards. <u>I'm</u> <u>serious</u>.

Life is a whole lot easier when you have options and skills to match the challenges that come up in daily life.

Having the mindset of *"I can do this"* will get you farther and get you better results than the *"I can't do this"* any day of the week.

The *"Can Do"* attitude is what every child has when they are born. The strength of that attitude will keep them breathing, eating, sleeping and making dirty diapers every day for those first few years. As they do these things, those babies begin to grow and learn.

Young children don't complain when they don't figure out how to do something the first time. They accept what is happening in the moment. They keep working and *doing* (not <u>trying</u>) and the results are obvious.

First, they just lay on the floor. Then they learn to turn over. Then, as muscles grow and skills are built, they can sit up, and then crawl, and then eventually after much effort and many attempts, they begin to walk.

Along the way, they didn't get depressed that it *wasn't working for them.* They worked through the *"failures"* and kept going.

There is a great man, very inspiring to me, by the name of Kirk Duncan and his company *3 Key Elements.* He has a great saying that I have taken to heart. It is: ***Hard Work + Faulty Philosophy = Frustration.*** If you are feeling frustrated, the best thing you can do is to get a better philosophy. The *"Can Do"* philosophy is a great place to start.

Confidence vs. Arrogance

Is there really a difference between these two? Tell you what, how about I give you the dictionary definition of each one.

<u>*Confidence*</u>: *the feeling or belief that one can rely on someone or something; firm trust.*

Ok, that's cool. Being able to rely on someone or something and having trust in that someone or something. Pretty straight forward on that definition, right? Let's look at Arrogance now.

Arrogance: *having or revealing an exaggerated sense of one's own importance or abilities*.

Well…that looks a bit different, doesn't it? So, arrogance is having or showing an <u>EXAGGERATED</u> sense of one's own abilities or how important they are. Ahhh…so they are a legend in their own mind and not in any one else's.

So what does this mean to us? Women love *confidence*. Sometimes they settle for *arrogance* and confuse it for *confidence*, or at least believe that *arrogance* is better than a complete wimp. And it's true.

Confidence is preferred every time that I have spoken to women to get their opinion. Having *confidence* is a firm trust in yourself. *Confidence* is also tied to a dominant personality and mindset.

Dominant doesn't have to mean *domineering*. It is quite different in reality.

Let's look at the definitions for these as well.

Dominant: *more important, powerful, or successful than most or all others*.

So, being confident in your abilities and what you can do can allow you to be *dominant* in your attitudes. It isn't about other people; it is an internal control and belief in yourself.

This is what being *dominant* means. It is an internal feeling and attitude.

Domineering: *assert one's will over another in an arrogant way.*

Now, this is the opposite of an internal feeling or attitude and the confidence that comes with it. *Domineering* is EXTERNAL!

It is forcing another person or people to do what you are wanting while having an exaggerated sense of how awesome you are.

Using the right words is so important to me. Using my language in this way is why I am so focused on what I want.

This is why I am specific in the words that I use and the attitude that I create and grow within myself. I am *confident* and *dominant*.

I choose to be this way. I wasn't always like this. It is a choice. You can make the choice too. The choice is yours.

Be Genuine

Have you ever tried to be someone else? Tried to be a *"cool guy"* or to fit into the *"in"* crowd? Did it work? Were you being the real you or was that simply an act?

We often will attempt to fit in with other people and groups to be accepted. Being something different and being perceived as *"better"* than we appear, is craved by nearly everyone.

The difference between the normal person *"trying"* to be someone else and the people who are *"doing"* it (*becoming someone better*) is that the person *"trying"* isn't being genuine.

Being genuine is being authentic. Being real. Not being authentic or real, means you are faking it and pretending to be something that is not truly a part of you.

When you stop making the effort, that part of you faking it doesn't continue. By being genuine and *"doing it,"* you change who you are and become more than you are right now.

All of your hopes, dreams, visions and goals that are focused on you becoming a better person are moving you towards a better life and version of reality than you were facing before. This is progress.

This is what every successful person in history has done. They have recognized their potential and realized that they had to change to *"become"* that new person. It wouldn't happen by itself and surely wouldn't happen overnight.

So now the question is: *What are you going to do about it?* You've read this book. You've seen, heard about, and read how this information has changed my life in many ways.

Being genuine is about being and becoming your authentic self. My authentic self is one who makes mistakes and yet keeps on moving forward. The equation for this is: **Hard Work + a Good Philosophy = Results**.

This helps my life to be fulfilled. Can you say the same? If so, welcome to your life. If not, you have a choice.

As Master Yoda said:

"Do, or do not. There is no try."

Your life is in your hands. You can choose to make it what you want it to be. If you have read this book and gotten this far, I think I know what your choice is. You are awesome. Live consciously and make your life the way you want it to be.

"The path we walk today comes from the actions we took yesterday.

The direction we go tomorrow is chosen by the actions we take today."

-Matthew Cooper

About the Author

Matthew Cooper is an expert communicator and entrepreneur. From a young age Matthew has always been curious about the world around him and as he got older that included people, and eventually women. Trained as a military Interrogator and Interpreter by the United States Army, he learned more about better ways to communicate with people around him and eventually leading him to purchasing a Crisis Intervention and Communication business in 2008 that he owns to this day.He has survived a divorce, got the kids, the house (selling that), and the dog (a.k.a.: *Cow*).

He currently resides in Salt Lake City, Utah with his five children and his *Jack Russell Terrier* Molly *"the Cow."*

He spends his time teaching workshops, doing private and group mentoring, continuing his martial arts studies and enjoying beautiful women wherever he meets them.

www.ingramcontent.com/pod-product-compliance
Lightning Source LLC
LaVergne TN
LVHW021506080426
835509LV00018B/2416